EATING GLASS

Learn more and sign up for my newsletter at www.markdjacobsen.com

EATING GLASS

*The Inner Journey
Through Failure and Renewal*

MARK D. JACOBSEN

Continual Ascent Books

Copyright (C) 2021 by Mark D. Jacobsen

All rights reserved. No part of this book may be reproduced in any manner whatsoever without written permission except in the case of brief quotations embodied in critical articles and reviews.

Cover design by Jess Estrella

The views expressed are those of the author and do not necessarily reflect the official policy or position of the Air Force, the Department of Defense, or the U.S. Government.

David Whyte, Mameen, from *River Flow: New and Selected Poems.* @2012 David Whyte, and *David Whyte: Essentials.* @2020 David Whyte. Excerpt reprinted with permission from Many Rivers Press, Langley, WA www.davidwhyte.com.

Version 2024.06

For Sam and John,
friends who saw me through

CONTENTS

Preface xv

INTRODUCTION 1

MY JOURNEY

WAR ROOMS 11
INSPIRATION 13
RISE 21
APEX 29
FALL 37
CRASH 45
EMBERS 53
RENEWAL 63

FAILING

THE FIRST STEP 71

VERTIGO	73
IDEAS	77
QUITTING	83
LONELINESS	87
IMPOSTOR SYNDROME	93
DOUBT	99
WEAKNESS	105
BURNOUT	111

AFTERMATH

OVER	119
HAS-BEEN	121
ANGER	127
HURT	131
SHARING	137
AFTERSHOCKS	143
FALSE STARTS	147
WILDERNESS	151

HEALING

HILL CLIMB	159
BEGINNING	161
HEALTH	165
PLAY	171
FRIENDSHIP	177
FAITH	183
SCARS	191

WAITING 197

RENEWAL

REINVENTION 205
FREEDOM 211
COURAGE 217
PRIORITIES 223
BOUNDARIES 229
GRATITUDE 235
PERSPECTIVE 241
POWER 247
LOVE 255

AFTERWORD 261
ACKNOWLEDGEMENTS 271

References 275

Recall the way you are all possibilities
you can see and how you live best
as an appreciator of horizons
whether you reach them or not.

Admit, that once you have got up
from your chair and opened the door,
once you have walked out into the clean air
toward that edge and taken the path up high
beyond the ordinary, you have become

the privileged and the pilgrim,
the one who will tell the story
and the one, coming back
from the mountain
who helped to make it.

        David Whyte, "Mameen"

*"Being an entrepreneur is like eating glass
and staring into the abyss of death."*

Elon Musk

PREFACE

For months, I debated whether to publish this book or bury it forever.

This book is about growing through failure. Specifically, it recounts my own experience of failure while attempting a daring moonshot project and struggling through my PhD. It also explores my inner journey through healing into a richer, wiser, and more centered life.

Publishing a book like this entails several dangers. In our age of personal branding, society expects us to project an image of success. Openly sharing our inner struggles violates a taboo, and a fine line separates authenticity and oversharing. There is also danger in identifying ourselves by our hardest life experiences, even if only for a season.

Time transforms how we understand hardship. In her book *The Rise*, Sarah Lewis writes that she deliberately avoids using the word *failure* because "once we begin to transform it, it ceases to be that any longer." We retroactively describe such an experience as "a learning experience, a trial, a reinvention."[1]

I agree with Lewis. Failure is never the last word, but rather a dynamic process that breaks us open and allows new life to shine forth. However, that retrospective alchemy is precisely why I felt the need to write this book. Failure does not transform overnight; this journey takes time, and honest accounts are rare. All too often the inner journey is, to borrow a phrase from the poet John Keats, writ in water.

However the world receives it, this book is the most vulnerable, true, and important thing I have ever written. Failure taught me precious lessons about life, and I choose to embrace that story—rather than hide it safely out of view—as I enter a new season of teaching, mentorship, and writing.

I ultimately decided to publish this book in order to help others. We all have experiences that shatter our sense of self and leave us gasping to breathe. The aftermaths of these experiences are rich seasons in which we can experience tremendous personal flourishing, but few of us are prepared for them or have trustworthy guides.

I have done my best to name the thoughts, feelings, and opportunities that accompany the journey through failure, because in naming a thing we gain power over it. What I ultimately hope for are empowered men and women who confidently embrace their stories to live more effectively and wholeheartedly in the world.

I must make two notes up front. First, I am not a mental health professional, and this book is only a tale of my own journey. When mental health struggles become serious, there is no substitute for experienced, professional help.

Second, I am acutely aware of my own privilege and would never dare to compare my experiences to the traumas, injustices, and oppression that so many in our world tragically face.

I will just say this: privilege does not armor us against the experience of personal failure. We are all human, we all struggle, and we all doubt ourselves and our place in this world.

During the years I wrote this book, two of my friends took their own lives. Both were successful, well-educated military officers who inspired and encouraged others. Yet both succumbed to inner battles they fought in secret. That was enough motivation for me to finish this book and release it into the world.

When I was at my worst, I took comfort in knowing that I was not alone. I treasured the writings of brave souls who told their raw, honest stories. They redeemed their failures by generously sharing their experiences. If this book can help others navigate their own inner journeys, I will be content.

Mark D. Jacobsen
January 13, 2021
Montgomery, AL

INTRODUCTION

We worry about fire every time we fly. Our nonprofit is developing drones for medical deliveries in conflict zones but Stanford's Lake Lagunita is a dry lakebed of crackling yellow grass and tangled, waist-high brush. We fly with a portable fire extinguisher, have discussed fire response procedures, and have rigorous safety processes, but I am always nervous. We have little choice. With the drought, all of northern California looks like this.

Today we are troubleshooting some new gremlin in the autopilot. We can recover by taking manual control, but today something else goes wrong. After a weak takeoff the plane inexplicably rolls to the right. The controls do not respond. Unable to hold altitude, the plane careens toward the ground. We see the impact and then a pillar of flame.

I dial 911 as I run. By the time we reach the crash site, the fire is the size of my house, billowing up in walls of flame when it encounters tangled brush. I run downwind with our portable fire extinguisher, hoping to halt the fire's advance, which is both futile and stupid. I deplete the extinguisher almost immediately, then gag on thick gray smoke and recoil from the searing heat.

We run to the two student dorms lying in the fire's path, yell, and pound on windows. Beyond those dorms are miles and miles of rolling hills, equally dead, equally yellow, equally flammable. If the fire escapes the lakebed, it will devour the open spaces cradling Silicon Valley.

I have never felt so helpless in my life. All we can do is watch Stanford burn. My heart leaps at the sound of sirens, but it is just a police car. The officer puts his hands on his hips and watches the fire. The flames lap at the perimeter road now. Branches overhanging the lakebed ignite. In minutes, the fire will escape the perimeter.

At last, a fire engine arrives, and then another. Firemen run and lay hoses. I can barely see them through the thick black smoke. I have no idea if they will contain the fire.

After identifying myself to the police, I sit on a log and wait. The firemen battle the blaze for two hours before they finally declare victory. Nobody is hurt. No buildings are destroyed. Three acres burned, but the fire will not devour the homes and open country behind Stanford.

With the immediate crisis over, something new comes: the weary, aching recognition that I have failed yet again.

This time, we will not recover.

It bothers my friends when I use the word *failure*.

You haven't failed, they tell me. You had setbacks. You made an amazing moonshot. So what if you didn't quite make it? You should be proud of what you accomplished. You laid groundwork others can build on.

Those are all true statements.

But I still failed.

For two years, that failure cast a long shadow over my life.

Even after that, the blows kept coming.

Fail fast, fail often, fail forward. That is the mantra in Silicon Valley.

We celebrate failure like Viking raiders toasting comrades fallen in glorious battle. We clank our frothy steins and hail their courage and honor. We weave epic tales of their battlefield prowess and the journeys of their immortal spirits to Valhalla. We yearn for a death half as good as our fallen heroes.

Any real warrior knows a battlefield death is not glorious. It is stupid mistakes, ill chance, screaming misery, urine and shit, fear and indignity. Dismembered youth strewn along the beach sob for their mothers.

We wrap battlefield death in legend not because it is so glorious, but because it is so terrible. We construct the legends, the myths, and the rituals so we can tame our own terror. Behind each of those gruff, bearded faces, a petrified child peers into the abyss of his own mortality. Will we have the courage to die so well? We clash our mugs, bellow at death, and applaud our own bravery.

Our modern world is not so different. We celebrate failure not because it is glorious, but because it is devastating. The vast majority of startups fail. If you peer behind the slick pitch decks and product prototypes, large numbers of entrepreneurs are tossing and turning in bed, wondering how to pay their employees when the cash runs out next month. They vomit in the toilet before meetings with VCs who might or might not give their dying company another three months of runway. Even as they proclaim world-changing solutions on tech blogs, terror and self-doubt tear their world asunder.

So we beat our chests and make our toasts. To Failure, that slayer of men and women who will rise again in eternity.

I recently listened to a sermon about failure. The pastor was emphatic: "I know you Silicon Valley people celebrate failure, but that's not what I'm talking about. It's not failure if you go on later to found a multimillion-dollar company. I'm talking about *failure*." That drew a hearty laugh, because everyone knew exactly what he meant.

And that's the rub. Our society celebrates failure, so long as it isn't really failure. Thousands of budding entrepreneurs will pay a fortune to hear Elon Musk or Jeff Bezos talk about failure. Our favorite stories are about indefatigable heroes who endured adversity after adversity before succeeding.

But God help you if your adversities seem to add up to nothing but a final, inglorious defeat. The crowds shy away because you are the thing they most fear becoming in their heart of hearts. You shake the foundations of their entire worldview. The story is not supposed to end this way.

If you have grit, you succeed. That is the tale we reassure ourselves with. But when it all comes apart, when it really does fail, when you have endured trial after trial only to end in nervous breakdown or bankruptcy? How could we ever dare greatly, if we live in a universe where such things might happen?

We pull the myth tighter around ourselves like a warm blanket.

And yet we continue to fail. Or to have setbacks, if you prefer. Our companies fold. We go bankrupt. We throw our half-finished novel into a bonfire and watch the pages blacken and curl. Our girlfriend drives away, glaring at us in the rearview mirror, and this time we know she's not coming back. Our career really is over because of a failed deal, bad luck, or that stupid, stupid thing we posted on Twitter. What the hell were we thinking?

Even as we celebrate what we have achieved, applaud ourselves for daring greatly, and shrug off failure, we are dying inside. Because nobody has really, honestly told us what failure *feels* like, and the truth is, it is terrifying and it is lonely and it hurts like hell.

We should start with definitions.

The simplest definition of failure is a lack of success. Our personal struggles often begin that way. Your moonshot misses. Your startup or small business crashes and burns. Your marriage falls apart. You return from Los Angeles or Nashville empty-handed after failing to make it as an actor or a songwriter.

My own struggle with failure began this way. My bold effort to break sieges in conflict zones and deliver humanitarian aid ultimately failed.

Yet the experience of failure goes so much deeper than a missed success. Failure can also mean a "state of inability to perform a normal function" or "fracturing or giving way under stress." Failure is a condition in which you pass beyond the limits of your strength into brokenness.

I once took an engineering class that involved stressing materials to failure. We placed solid metal rods in powerful machines that twisted, compressed, and pulled until thundering *cracks* made us jump behind our safety glasses. An entire discipline of failure theory studies "the conditions under which solid materials fail under the action of external loads."

Now we're talking.

When you struggle with failure, specific events in your life, job, or relationships usually serve as proximate causes. They stretch and torque and compress you as a human being. All of us learn to tolerate setbacks, challenges, and even failures. But there comes a point when the external stresses overwhelm our capacities. Our souls fracture.

This experience of personal failure appears to be endemic. References to therapists, yogis, and Buddhist mentors pepper interviews with startup founders and corporate executives. Conferences devoted to celebrating failure charge a fortune and quickly sell out. Entrepreneurs share their stories of failure and crisis on anonymous websites. Dr. Michael Freeman found that 49% of entrepreneurs have one or more mental health conditions, with 30% reporting depression.[2] Studies have also found a striking mental health crisis in graduate education, with 30-40% of PhD candidates reporting moderate to severe anxiety or depression.[3] Teen suicides plague Palo Alto, the heart of Silicon Valley.[4] These communities include some of the most successful people in the world, and they are barely holding it together.

Yet for all this apparent need, most high achievers still battle their demons in private. References are veiled and clipped. Many high achievers refuse to show any hint of trouble at all.

Stanford students use the metaphor of a duck; they appear to bob placidly along the smooth surface, but underneath they are paddling furiously to survive. In high-success cultures we learn to show no weakness. We become phenomenal actors.

When I initiate conversations about failure with others, their defenses typically come down just enough that I glimpse a secret battle they have never dared to reveal. Then the shields go back up and I'm left wondering if I imagined the whole thing.

Maybe I'm wrong.

Maybe everyone else is fine.

Maybe it's just me.

But I don't think it's just me. It's not just you.

We all have seasons when failure destroys our sense of self and rips our world asunder. We carry our pain like Frodo trudging toward Mordor with his shoulders sagging beneath the insufferable weight of the ring. No one else can carry that burden. No one else can understand. In many cases, no one else can even know.

Too many of us suffer in silence. Our world is finally beginning to have open conversations about failure. Unfortunately, many of these conversations breeze past the pain; we jump right to learning, iterating, and failing our way to success. Missing is an honest exploration of what failure is like *while you are going through it.*

When we fail, we cannot jump immediately to redemption.

INTRODUCTION

Failure is a process. Healing takes time, but so does failing. Failure can last months, as relationships unravel, the market changes, cash burns away, setbacks accumulate, or the lawyers hammer out the divorce agreement.

We will get to healing, growth, and new life. We will reflect on how failure forges our souls. We will remind ourselves that any successful human being—whether she is an entrepreneur, president, Olympic athlete, novelist, or devoted mother—will leave a trail of setbacks and failures along the way. We will come to recognize that failure tempers us like steel.

But that is not where we must start.

Right now we are riding out a storm. Waves of seawater crash over the deck, the masts splinter, the sails rip. We careen through the dark and the rain, clutching whatever line or plank we can find, and take our bearings with each white flash of lightning. We cannot even begin to think about swimming ashore. That comes later. For now, we have to survive. And when the waves subside and the roiling black clouds recede on the horizon, it takes time to find our way back to civilization. We cannot rush that process, because that is where the most growth occurs, in all its terrible beauty.

That is what many conversations about failure miss. That is what I'm writing about.

PART ONE

MY JOURNEY

WAR ROOMS

Across the street from St. James Park in London, a nondescript staircase descends beneath the streets of Westminster. A passerby might mistake it for a Tube station, were it not for the sign overhead. Its modest appearance belies its significance to the history of Great Britain, and indeed the world.

Descend those stairs and you travel back in time. Crinkled maps of Europe plaster the pale walls, while sheaves of yellowed papers and brightly colored rotary phones cover the tables. The rooms appear exactly as they did when British Prime Minister Sir Winston Churchill used them to lead the war effort against Nazi Germany.

The War Rooms are a hallowed place. When I visited after graduating from the U.S. Air Force Academy, I passed through each room in reverent silence. I could only imagine what Winston Churchill felt during those long years, carrying the weight of western civilization on his shoulders.

In one of the final rooms, just before returning to a world of busy Londoners and dazzling sunlight, a visitor to the War Rooms comes across this quote:

I felt as if... all my life had been but a preparation for this hour and for this trial.

Emotion overcame me. I was young, fresh out of the Academy, my life before me a blank canvas. Questions of passion, meaning, and destiny haunted me. As a devout Christian, I believed God had a great purpose in store for me. I dreamed of changing the world but did not know where to begin.

Churchill's words offered hope that someday, maybe decades from now, all the disparate parts of my life might come together. Perhaps someday I too could look back on my life and reverently whisper, "it all prepared me for *this*."

Perhaps I too would have a finest hour.

INSPIRATION

My dream was born in Istanbul.

It was an appropriate place because the city bridges worlds. East and West, Christianity and Islam, ancient and modern, meet in its streets. Civilizations layer the city. Peeling Islamic calligraphy in the Hagia Sophia mosque exposes Byzantine Christian paintings, and the crumbling city walls record history like epic tree rings. Istanbul, like the rest of Turkey, teeters between two visions of political order. Europe and a rich Islamic past both beckon.

The past and future seem equally alive in Istanbul. The weight of history surrounds you, but the city is a place of boundless possibility.

It is a city in which to reflect, sense one's place in the story of human civilization, and imagine entirely new futures.

On March 10, 2014 I was in Istanbul researching the Syrian civil war when the United Nations Relief and Works Agency (UNRWA) released a staggering photograph.[5] A haggard crowd of thousands vanishes into the glare of white light, surrounded on either side by crumbling buildings, buckled concrete, and exposed rebar. It looks like Stalingrad.

The place is Yarmouk, a Palestinian refugee camp in the suburbs of Damascus, and one of the first cities in Syria to experience the Assad regime's "surrender or starve" tactics. These Syrians wait in line for a rare food delivery after three months of siege.

Their faces show a mix of despair and iron resolution. Some crane their necks to see above the crowd, wondering if their turn will ever come. A man in a black jacket stares at the ground, shoulders slumped, perhaps too ashamed to look up. Farther back, a slouching man stares into the camera, one hand upturned, lips parted as if he wishes to say something. He might be making a silent plea to the photographer, or an accusation.

The photo went viral. It appeared on the cover of an Amnesty International report about sieges in Syria. Activists displayed it in Times Square in New York.

Skeptics claimed the photo was a forgery. It was not. The world simply could not believe that such atrocities still occurred in the 21st century.

The Syrian civil war began with a peaceful uprising that the world has largely forgotten. Inspired by protests in other Arab countries, Syrians took to the streets to demand dignity, a better life, and freedom from corrupt authoritarian rule. The regime met these protestors with bullets, paramilitary brutality, torture, and permanent "disappearances."

After months of state violence, defectors from the Syrian army took up arms against their murderous government. The insurgency exploded in February 2012 when the regime began a month-long artillery bombardment of Homs. Every town and village seemed to stand up its own rebel group in the ensuing months. Islamists poured in from abroad.

By the time I visited Turkey a year later, civil war had engulfed Syria. We met with opposition leaders, journalists, rebel commanders, and activists. They were desperate, confused, and badly fragmented. They knew they were losing. Their political leaders had failed them. Jihadists were outmaneuvering more moderate factions. The West declined to get involved. Every meeting had an air of desperation.

The opposition needed a miracle. Some hoped for a full-scale American intervention. Others called for an ill-defined program of American support for what remained of the Free Syrian Army. Syrians wanted the West to know that they weren't terrorists. They only wanted freedom and dignity, but now warred against a monstrous regime that tortured and raped and starved its people.

The brutality of the Syrian civil war was staggering.

We met a woman who had survived both a chemical attack and a siege. The siege was worse, she said. Watching your children starve, knowing you can do nothing.

One evening we dined with a U.S. diplomat who talked at length about the siege of Yarmouk. His team had explored every option to deliver aid, he said. Ground convoys, airdrops, even catapults. No aid could get in.

After dinner I overheard a Syrian activist named Hind venting to her friends. "The U.S. Air Force can do whatever it wants," she seethed. "America doesn't *want* to help."

I felt compelled to speak up because I happened to be a U.S. Air Force C-17 cargo pilot. I told Hind that even the U.S. Air Force wasn't invincible. Flying cargo aircraft into the middle of heavily defended airspace against the host government's will was impossible. The Syrian regime would shoot down planes unless the U.S. destroyed the entire air defense system first. That would not happen, because the U.S. feared entanglement in the Syrian war.

Hind appreciated my perspective. She could not argue with an Air Force pilot.

We continued on to our hotel, feeling frustrated and helpless.

That night I couldn't sleep.

I felt a deep personal connection to the Middle East. In addition to serving as a cargo pilot, I had spent a year learning Arabic at the Defense Language Institute and two years earning a master's degree in Jordan. My wife Wendy and I were living in Amman when the Arab Spring began, and we felt the pain of our Arab friends when the Syrian crisis escalated into civil war. I now studied at the Air Force's prestigious School of Advanced Air & Space Studies (SAASS), researching complex, multi-sided civil wars. SAASS had generously supported and funded my research trip.

I lay awake contemplating the sieges. I felt the weight of responsibility. As a Major, I had little authority. Nonetheless, finding a way to deliver badly needed cargo in a war zone was part of my job—especially as a cargo pilot and Middle East specialist. Telling Hind "no" seemed inadequate. In the 21st century, feeding a besieged city had to be possible.

I tossed and turned. My mind raced. I tried out alternatives, discarding them as fast as they emerged.

Then lightning struck.

If we couldn't fly one big airplane through Syria's air defenses, maybe we could fly a lot of little planes. I imagined an army of ants stealing a picnic lunch.

The requisite technologies were advancing rapidly. The same technology used in cell phones had ignited a revolution in small drones. Batteries stored more power and lasted longer. Computer chips, GPS receivers, and inertial sensors were smaller and lighter. Powerful, inexpensive drone autopilots had hit the market.

I envisioned several possible ways to build an air bridge into Yarmouk. Quadcopters. Fixed-wing drones. Balloons. Airships. Cheap gliders launched from cargo planes over Jordan or Turkey.

An effort like this would need a team, but I was plugged into all the right networks: air mobility pilots, logisticians, Middle East specialists, U.S. embassies in the region, the Air Force's professional strategist community, the defense innovation sector, Syrian activists, humanitarian organizations.

We would need to do a ton of research. Flight ranges of drones. Energy density of batteries. Distances to besieged areas from neighboring countries. Besieged population sizes, required calorie counts, and the mass of daily food required. Balloon diameters for various payload sizes, using either helium or hydrogen.

My mind whirled in overdrive.

This would be unbelievably hard but it was *possible*.

Sometime after midnight, I got out a flashlight and a notebook and started working.

I didn't stop for a year and a half.

That morning we flew to Gaziantep, a city in eastern Turkey that served as a hub for aid going into Syria. Later the Islamic State in Iraq and Sham (ISIS) infiltrated the city, making it too dangerous for most Westerners. After two days in Gaziantep we traveled to Reyhanli, a stone's throw from the Syrian border, where I looked out my hotel window at idling lorries waiting to cross through congested checkpoints. Mortar fire periodically rumbled over the hills. Turkish intelligence stopped our bus, suspicious of our identities and intentions.

Our meetings with Syrians became more intense. We met a Syrian doctor named Waliid who had lost most of his family to airstrikes and President Assad's prisons; he still rushed to the sound of explosions to aid the wounded. His story left most of us in tears. We met a young married couple, Sunni and Alawite, who risked their lives to smuggle medical supplies through regime checkpoints. We visited fly-by-night aid organizations where workers raged at the biggest aid organizations—like the UN and

Red Cross—for primarily serving regime-held areas in Syria.

We confronted the war's moral complexity. We visited a hospital where wounded Syrian fighters tried to impress us with cell phone images of heads they had severed. We inadvertently found ourselves in an administrator's office with two low-ranking members of Jebhat al-Nusra, the Syrian branch of al-Qa'eda. A girl told us of watching her best friend paraded naked through her village and raped against a tank. We visited an orphanage filled with glass-eyed children who did not laugh, smile, or play. Later, we learned that regime soldiers had systematically executed the adult men in their village in front of them. We met a revolutionary who used his college tuition money to found a rebel battalion. ISIS annihilated his men and he escaped to Turkey.

We processed our emotions in different ways. Many needed to talk. We met late each night to debrief the day's events. Students shed tears and asked hard questions.

I coped by working.

Between meetings I sketched ideas and researched technical details. I filled my notebook with basic calculations, lists of potential stakeholders, and details of promising companies. I built maps in Google Earth, measured distances, and calculated glide ratios.

I talked late into each night with a colleague who ran an aid organization active in Syria. He and other Syrians I met loved the idea, which seemed to validate my hypothesis that an air bridge would add value. If we could just build the planes, he would coordinate the first airdrops inside Syria.

That was our moonshot: one package onto the roof of a Syrian hospital. That historic milestone would prove an entirely new paradigm for dealing with wartime sieges.

We called our effort the Syria Airlift Project.

INSPIRATION

My brief exposure to the Syrian war changed me.

On the long flight home to Alabama, I re-watched *Lincoln*. In the final scene, Lincoln delivers his second inaugural address:

> With malice toward none, with charity for all, with firmness in the right as God gives us to see the right, let us strive on to finish the work we are in, to bind up the nation's wounds, to care for him who shall have borne the battle and for his widow and his orphan, to do all which may achieve and cherish a just and lasting peace among ourselves and with all nations.

I buried my face in my jacket, pretended to sleep, and silently cried out the emotions of the past eight days.

After my return, I struggled to communicate what I had experienced. During a presentation to my military colleagues at SAASS, I broke down in tears. My peers stared with awe and incomprehension.

My quiet suburban life felt vacuous compared to the life-or-death drama unfolding in Syria.

I have since met many people who brushed with Syria.

It changed all of us.

Unlike most people who watch such horrors from afar, I was in a position to do something that might save lives.

I thought of Churchill's War Rooms.

Every thread of my life seemed to converge in this project. I flew cargo planes in the U.S. Air Force. I spoke fluent Syrian Arabic and held a degree from the University of Jordan. I had helped found an organization called the Defense Entrepreneurs Forum, which promoted disruptive innovation inside the Department of Defense. I had degrees in Astronautical Engineering, International Relations, Conflict Resolution, and Strategy. I had grown up building robots with my dad and worked throughout high school at his hobby store. I had even learned some Turkish, thinking it might be useful in my Syria research. I was about to begin a PhD at Stanford, where I would have access to some of the best talent in the world. I had dreamed of becoming an entrepreneur, but never knew how, especially while I was still in the military.

My eclectic skill set had never gone anywhere. Demand for Arabic-speaking cargo pilots with astronautical engineering degrees was low.

Suddenly, all that mattered immensely.

RISE

How do you begin the impossible?

They say the journey of a thousand miles begins with the first step, but the first step is rarely obvious. Imagine standing at the base of Everest, hands on your hips, peering with craned neck up into the clouds. You know you must begin somewhere, but starting up the mountain now would be fatal.

You have choices to make. Mentors to seek. Research to conduct. Gear to buy. Skills to acquire. Strength to build. The choices multiply in a combinatorial explosion. The immensity and open-endedness of the challenge is overwhelming. The fear of a wrong move paralyzes you.

Who are you to dare this?

And yet you need to do something.

So you do your best.

You pick that first step.

And you begin.

I cringe when I recall my first steps.

We needed a team, so I emailed everyone in my network who had relevant knowledge or skills. I set up a project management site, sent out invites, and watched enthusiastic volunteers pour in. We quickly hit 50 members. I sent daily updates, assigned research tasks, and drove discussions.

The first week was exhilarating. The second week, message

traffic fell by half. By the third week, I was mostly talking to myself. I shut down the site and started over with the handful of active contributors.

I knew little about drones so emailed everybody I could find with relevant experience: college students who made the news with a burrito-delivering drone, a San Francisco startup that promised drone delivery of prescription medications, a YouTuber who designed custom planes out of Dollar Tree foam board. I barraged them with questions.

In retrospect, my ignorance was appalling. I told them I wanted an aircraft capable of delivering 50 pounds. I gradually learned that goal was outrageous. Later, we pared our goal down to five pounds, then two. Even that pushed the state of the art. My emails must have sounded amateurish, which they were.

But I got replies. And slowly, I learned.

I bought a radio-controlled plane and an autopilot.

I never expected we would build our own drones; we would need to find a partner organization for that. However, I believed in getting one's hands dirty. When you fully immerse yourself in a new domain, see things with your own eyes, and hold technology in your own hands, you gain insights you never would otherwise.

I felt sick with dread the first time I sent that plane into the air. Amazingly, the plane stayed airborne. With each orbit around the field, my confidence grew. Eventually I got cocky and tried a loop. The subsequent crash sheared the motor off the mount.

I waited a week for replacement parts. I learned about glue.

The next time I flew, I busted all my propellers. I waited another week for replacements.

When the autopilot and accessories arrived, I learned hard lessons about connectors. Nothing fit together. An angry night of googling revealed that the RC world used a gazillion mutually incompatible connectors. I ordered wire cutters, more connectors, and a new soldering iron.

Months passed this way. I spent two maddening nights troubleshooting the ground control station, only to discover that key features weren't implemented yet. I had baud rate problems. A defective GPS unit. Prop spinners the wrong diameter. Weight and CG problems. Wingtip stalls. Stripped servos. Most fly days ended in a rapid crash and a week or two of repairs or waiting for parts.

It was absolute hell.

Any worthwhile endeavor awakens a malevolent force that Steven Pressfield calls Resistance.[6] It is as certain as death and taxes. Resistance will thwart your ambitions, shatter your dreams, break your spirit, and leave you to slink off into addiction or tired mediocrity—unless you fight. Overcoming Resistance is the great battle of any creative person's life.

From the day I started the Syria Airlift Project, I warred against Resistance. I struggled to build a team. Few people believed in the project. The engineering was insanely difficult. Each step forward gave us five more problems to solve. Every setback sent me into an emotional tailspin.

I refused to give up.

At the end of my worst days, I pulled my dog-eared copies of Pressfield's books off the shelf and reread his passages about battling Resistance. I journaled. I translated every failure into a list of lessons learned. I reminded myself that every failure provided an opportunity to learn.

My wife Wendy and I lived and breathed Syria. Wendy also spoke Arabic and had a passion for the region after our years in Jordan. We had Syrian friends. When we watched our three small children sleep, we thought back to that horrific photo of the bread line in Yarmouk. Children were dying this very night in Aleppo and

Hama and Homs. Sieges continued to unfold throughout Syria and would only get worse.

I was in a position to do something.

That was enough motivation to keep fighting.

When you stand your ground before Resistance, the universe responds with a countervailing force that Pressfield calls Assistance.

I met Daniel at the local RC flying park. He was a quirky loner who spent lazy days chain smoking beside his truck. Every half hour or so he would rise from his camp chair, grind his cigarette butt into the grass, and launch an RC plane. Five or ten exhilarating minutes would follow, and then he would put the dead battery on the charger, settle back into his chair, and light up again. Daniel took an interest in my work and gave me small pointers. His presence and simple friendship infused me with strength.

Assistance arrived again a month later when I stalled my thousand-dollar fixed-wing drone over a tree line. It vanished into the canopy with a sickening crunch. Daniel whistled grimly. I spent hours trudging through snarled underbrush, listening to the periodic heartbeat of the drone somewhere above. I couldn't spot it amidst the impossibly thick foliage.

This was a devastating setback. I had already poured a personal fortune into the work. I couldn't afford to replace this drone.

My friend Zach, a hunter and experienced tree climber, learned that I needed help. He made three separate trips out to the field with tree-climbing gear, bamboo poles, and duct tape, climbing to potentially fatal heights until he found and recovered the drone.

This act of selfless generosity overwhelmed me.

I had rarely been reduced to such dependency. Letting go, and entrusting myself to others, felt dangerous and exhilarating.

Shortly after that crash, I graduated from SAASS and moved to California. SAASS had chosen me for the rare privilege of earning an Air Force-sponsored PhD, with a commitment to eventually join SAASS faculty. I planned to spend two months of leave with family in Napa before beginning my studies at Stanford. That meant two months to surge on the Syria Airlift Project.

The disasters continued.

My first week in Napa, I visited the local RC airfield. Two friendly pilots came over to say hello. The first flight went well, although I landed hard. On my second takeoff my plane lurched abruptly to the left, straight at my new friends, its ten-inch propeller whirling at several thousand RPM. They dove for their lives.

I discovered afterwards that the first hard landing had cocked the motor mount askew. I apologized profusely but their mistrust was palpable. I was too humiliated to go back.

I began flying at a local park instead. Every morning at 5:30 am I lugged my gear up a hillside to a picnic table overlooking acres of vineyards. Nothing worked right. Every flight was erratic. Strange bugs occurred. My GPS would not acquire a lock. I worried about fire. Joggers watched me suspiciously, and a woman complained that I scared her dog.

I was learning, but too slowly.

I finally moved to Stanford.

Here was one of the greatest concentrations of technical talent in the United States. Here I would find brilliant, big thinkers who wanted to change the world. Here, finally, I could build a team.

The best place to fly was Lake Lagunita, the dry lakebed planted in the middle of campus where Stanford's drone club operated. I couldn't have asked for a better site. It was huge and only five minutes from my new home.

I visited at my first opportunity.

I preflighted my plane, armed the motor, and threw the plane into the air.

The ground station immediately blared a warning: FENCE BREACH.

I felt a horrible sense of vertigo. The plane had entered an automatic failsafe mode and ignored my frantic efforts to take over. It shot towards the horizon, becoming fainter and smaller until it disappeared entirely. The vertigo turned to dread.

I had just experienced what drone pilots call a "flyaway." Later, I learned that a combination of three separate software bugs in the ground station software caused the malfunction. I had not flown this particular plane since SAASS, and it erroneously thought it was still supposed to be in Alabama. When it found itself airborne in California, it activated a geofence failsafe and embarked on a cross-country flight home.

The plane was spinning a heavy ten-inch prop at thousands of RPM through hilly terrain where hikers roamed. A strike could be fatal. Trembling, I drove to the foothills. I hiked for hours, lugging around the ground station laptop and an antenna, listening for an electronic heartbeat. Nothing. My best estimate is that the plane flew approximately 20 miles over the densest part of Silicon Valley at roughly 500 feet, passing between two major airports, before its batteries died and it glided to a crash landing. My name and phone number were taped inside.

I sat trembling on the sofa most of the evening, waiting for the police to knock on the door. Wendy and I made contingency plans in case I went to jail.

The knock never came.

After two or three days, I began to breathe again.

"You don't have enough experience," Wendy told me. "You're going to hurt somebody. You need a partner."

I promised not to fly again until I found one.

I met Brandon through the Stanford drone club. He was an experienced RC pilot languishing several years into a Mechanical Engineering PhD program. His grueling PhD experience had damaged his self-confidence, and he was questioning both his abilities and his life trajectory. The Syria Airlift Project infused him with purpose.

We began to fly together each weekend.

After more than five months of struggling, I was no longer alone.

Assistance had arrived again.

A team was born.

In October, I pitched the Syria Airlift Project at an innovation competition. I was a nervous wreck going in, but once I took the stage, blazing self-confidence took over. We won the competition, garnering $3,000. The third-place finalist donated his own cash prize. After months of spending my own money, the prize money gave us a lifeline.

An even bigger prize came a few days later, in the form of a phone call from Jessie Mooberry, an exuberant Quaker pacifist who spoke at the conference. She wanted to volunteer. Within days, she scheduled meetings with humanitarian organizations in D.C. and New York. Over the next few months, Jessie stood up a nonprofit called Uplift Aeronautics to run the Syria Airlift Project. Uplift became our new identity.

Word spread. Our project appeared before a UN panel on humanitarian drones. The media reached out. Uplift appeared in everything from the Washington Post to the leading magazines for technical hobbyists.

A colleague at Air Force Headquarters briefed the project to the Chief of Staff, the highest ranking general in the U.S. Air Force. This was a critical development; I had always viewed our project as an Air Force contribution that the U.S. could employ in humanitarian crises. We only organized as a nonprofit out of necessity, but for the paradigm to survive, it would *have* to transition into the Air Force. The Chief apparently loved the work but no help ever came of the meeting.

Our team grew. We attracted a top-notch law student who helped tackle the complex legal issues in play, as well as a Syrian engineer studying in the U.S. Other Stanford students began to help.

Our vision was no longer just a dream. We had a team, a little funding, and growing external support. The Syria Airlift Project actually stood a chance.

APEX

Uplift's rapid ascent was exhilarating, but Brandon and I were overwhelmed. We were both full-time PhD students at one of the most demanding universities in the world. Worse, the Air Force only gave me three years to complete a program that took most students six. I would be reassigned after those three years, which meant I faced immense pressure to both finish my PhD and transition Uplift's work into the Air Force or another entity.

I had sailed through every school in my life, but my PhD classes crushed me. Worse, my research proposals floundered with my faculty. I wanted to leverage a scientific paradigm called complexity theory, which had transformed other academic disciplines but barely touched Political Science. I met stiff resistance. I also wanted to study armed groups in Syria, but one of the department's most distinguished professors told me I could not study Syria because of data challenges. I was aghast at a philosophy of science that fenced off the world's most urgent contemporary problems because they weren't conducive to fashionable methods of inquiry.

I failed to build a single meaningful relationship with anyone on faculty that year. I had no idea who might serve as a dissertation advisor. Every research idea felt like a dead end. The three-year deadline approached like a slow-motion train wreck. My stress mounted, the first twisting and straining towards personal failure.

I achieved good grades and took my comprehensive exams a

semester early, but my faculty saw me as hopelessly distracted. No one supported the Syria Airlift Project or even showed interest. One professor refused to let me miss a single class to attend a humanitarian conference, where I was scheduled to present. I went anyway, securing a $40,000 grant while there. I permanently lost his trust.

Brandon was in a similar position. He overcommitted to the Syria Airlift Project, fell behind in his studies, and found himself on shaky ground with his advisor.

Still, the Syria Airlift Project was succeeding. We had to press ahead.

Because we studied full-time, we struggled to advance Uplift's goals during Stanford's hectic ten-week quarters. We sometimes flew on weekends, but our roadmap mostly involved surging during breaks.

Over Christmas break we planned to focus on airdrop capability at long ranges. During spring break I wanted to conduct a major demonstration in California involving Syrian refugees. If that gained us enough support, we would try to replicate the demonstration in Turkey over the summer. That would give us everything we needed to make our first flight across the border into Syria—if we could just convince the right authorities. Maybe then we could transition the project to another organization.

On the other hand, if we could not get to Turkey in the summer, we would probably need to abandon the effort. Brandon and I could not afford to give the project another year.

The pressure was on.

Christmas break was exhilarating. Jessie flew out to join us. We laid out our vision and goals for the nonprofit. We continued to struggle with technical setbacks but also began crossing milestones: consistent, reliable flights, automated takeoffs from a bungee launcher, package airdrops, a simultaneous flight of two drones, and a 50-kilometer flight. Later, we achieved 100 kilometers. A drone company donated thousands of dollars of hardware, enabling us to build a new drone fleet. After the months of failure, these successes felt amazing.

We didn't have time to congratulate ourselves.

Spring break was fast approaching. If we wanted to conduct a major demonstration, we needed to prepare now.

Brandon and I did not feel ready. We were rushing the engineering. We needed bigger, more capable planes for the demo. Jessie urged us to go big; this was a make-or-break moment, and we would not have another chance.

I knew she was right.

We made the gamble.

A Syrian friend of mine led an Arab refugee center in Sacramento. I suggested we partner to run a Refugee Empowerment Event, in which we would teach refugees to operate several planes for humanitarian deliveries. We would show the world this project was not simply about flying drones, but about empowering refugees to bring aid and healing back to their country.

We ordered four new, larger planes. This was a huge risk. Preparing a new type of aircraft required considerable work and we had no idea how well it would perform. We christened this aircraft the "Waliid," named for the heroic doctor I had met in Turkey.

Finding a location to host the event proved to be our hardest challenge. Whenever we mentioned Syria and drones, institutions recoiled. Syria conjured up images of terrorism and war. In some cases, it evoked fears of Arabs and Muslims; the "flying bomb" scenario crossed everyone's mind. Even progressive organizations fretted over liability. We called everyone we could think of, including civil airports, universities, and farms. Nobody would support the event.

My stress mounted with each passing day. For the first time in my life, I had consistent trouble sleeping.

The stakes kept rising. A veteran BBC film crew learned about our event. I warned them that I could not guarantee success, but they insisted on flying out from the United Kingdom. A world-leading drone company planned to send several engineers.

The lack of a suitable location became a crisis. Desperate, Wendy and I jumped in the car one Saturday to personally visit three RC airfields in Sacramento. One club refused to even meet with us; they suspected nefarious intent, raised doubts about whether I was even in the Air Force, and spread rumors that we were up to no good. A second club got word and brushed us off.

At the third club we finally found an ally. Just two weeks before the event, Norman—the club president—agreed we could use his field. We breathed a huge sigh of relief.

Eight days prior to the event, Norman sent me a devastating email. His club members had mutinied when they learned about the event. They had convened an emergency meeting behind his back in order to vote. Our prospects didn't look good, but he said I could attend the meeting to plead my case.

Resistance was back with a vengeance.

So was my insomnia.

Jessie and I rehearsed the entire two-hour drive to the meeting. Our reception was cold. Jessie did a masterful job thawing the audience before the meeting officially started. It didn't hurt that she was charismatic, earning her private pilot's license, and female.

I gave my talk everything I had. I showcased my Air Force service. I talked about our country's foreign policy struggles in the Middle East and our opportunity to do something in the world that America could be proud of. I evoked the memory of the Berlin Airlift. I asked them to give us a chance.

The vote passed 11-9.

After the vote, Norman met us in the parking lot. He explained that he had been an Army Ranger in Vietnam. He had seen and done things he was not proud of. He believed in what we were trying to do, using airplanes to bring some good into the world.

There was just one more thing, he said.

You'd better not fuck this up.

That remained a grave concern.

Waliid, our new plane, was still not ready. Brandon had worked around the clock to modify the airframe for payload delivery. One week before the event, he finished the first plane. The craftsmanship was exquisite. But would it fly? We had such poor success with many of our previous planes.

We took Waliid 1 out that afternoon for trials. It flew remarkably well at first, but then tragedy struck. On one takeoff, the bungee launcher failed to disconnect from the plane. When it went taut, it dragged the plane back into the ground at maximum speed, where it caught fire.

The plane had crashed in a marshy patch of the lakebed, and the fire mercifully fizzled out in a puddle. However, Waliid 1 was wrecked. The fuselage had broken in two, and the burning speed controller had badly charred the aft section. I could only stare.

We were one week out from the event and did not have a flyable airplane. We were failing, with the BBC reporters arriving the next day and world-leading drone engineers watching over our shoulders. I was scheduled to speak about the project at the Embedded Linux conference in San Jose the next day.

That night I returned to Lake Lagunita, alone. The lakebed was still and cool and quiet, ringed by silhouetted trees.

I sat in the grass, looked out over the moonlit lakebed, and broke down in tears.

We were failing. We had tried so hard, invested so much, and achieved so many milestones. It all culminated in this moment, but without Waliid flying reliably, the event would flop. We would share our vision and throw a few small planes in the air to entertain the children, but it would be a disaster. BBC would go home empty-handed. We would be a laughingstock.

I had never known a failure of this magnitude in my life.

In the morning, after another night of tormented sleep, I received a text from Tomoki, an undergraduate volunteer on the project.

I fixed it.

I did not understand. I met Tomoki at his dorm, where he showed me the miracle he had wrought. He had painstakingly reconstructed Waliid 1's fuselage, replaced the speed controller, and returned the plane to a flyable condition.

The universe had delivered Assistance again.

That afternoon I spoke at the Embedded Linux conference, to an audience that included the "who's who" of the drone engineering community. We had been courting some of these developers for months. They loved what they heard and wanted to help. Our project tended to inspire engineers, who longed to use their skills for good but had no idea how.

We showed off Waliid 1. When I told the story of the crash and the miraculous reconstruction, the audience laughed in approval.

Brandon redesigned the defective bungee hook, and our test flights went perfectly.

Waliid was flying.

Our team members flew in from around the country. The BBC film crew arrived. My good friend Brian, a professional videographer, flew in from Seattle to shoot a fundraising video.

We were exhausted from the Stanford winter quarter but also bristling with energy. We felt like we were heading into the Super Bowl.

Our Refugee Empowerment Event would be the last two days of spring break, which gave us several days to prepare. We worked around the clock, doing final engineering in the mornings and then test flights in the afternoons.

I still felt sick with anxiety.

Two days before the main event, everything came together perfectly: flight after flight, each one flawless, each one delivering a 1kg payload bundle. We wouldn't feed a city this way, but we could deliver high-value, low-mass medical supplies to hospitals that the Syrian regime continually besieged and bombed. Our Syrian partner organizations told us this would meet a real need.

I was delirious with relief.

Wendy ordered us a takeout dinner. As the sun set over Lake Lagunita, we gathered family-style around picnic tables to share a meal. For a few minutes the pressure was off, and we ate and laughed and talked. This remains my single favorite memory from the project: sharing a family dinner together and seeing that we had built a real team.

That Friday we bought food, filled coolers, rented generators, and loaded up U-Hauls. The next morning, we rose at dawn, headed to the airfield, and set up. We were ready for action when our Arab volunteers arrived, looking unsure of what they had signed up for.

I welcomed them in Arabic and then we got right to work explaining the airplanes and how they worked. We taught our volunteers how to run preflight inspections and then formed groups to walk through the pre-flight checklists and launch sequence.

Once the first plane launched and the first package parachuted down, our volunteers finally grasped what we were trying to do. They were enthralled.

We launched plane after plane. The children decorated the airdrop boxes with hearts, animals, and messages for Syria. A group of women made parachutes out of garbage bags and string.

When we started airdropping candy, the excitement reached a crescendo. Kids laughed and screamed and ran about as candy rained down from the sky. I had borrowed the idea from the Berlin Airlift of 1948. A year of grueling work had gone into creating this magical experience, and I looked away to hide my tears. I could only dream about recreating this perfect moment for children in Syria.

That night we slept in a massive rental house that Wendy had found online. We ate another family dinner, held a rushed board meeting, and then shared a big pancake breakfast in the morning. We did the whole performance again on Sunday, with a larger group.

The event was a remarkable success.

Afterwards, I gathered our group and tried to hold myself together while I expressed my pride and gratitude for all that they had accomplished. Recreating this event in Turkey would be our next major goal. If we could do it here, I told them, we could do it there.

We drove home happy but utterly drained.

Stanford's spring quarter started the next morning.

FALL

Every trajectory has its apogee: that moment of weightless transcendence in which you marvel at the heights to which you have soared. There you hang, motionless, frozen for one perfect instant in the utter stillness between rise and fall, somewhere between the earth and the stars. You turn silently in light and shadow. Awestruck.

And then you are falling.

The success in Sacramento masked deep problems.

First, our health was rapidly deteriorating. Exhaustion, anxiety, and insomnia haunted me now. I prided myself on my ability to shoulder superhuman workloads, but I was badly burned out. Although I was still on track to finish my PhD program in the allotted three years, I could no longer give the nonprofit the lion's share of my time and energy.

Second, we found no support among key organizations and people whose help we desperately needed. I naively hoped for Air Force support and sought it every way I knew how. Although Air Force leadership applauded my work, that never translated into action. I briefed the project widely but only one general ever bothered to contact me. I replied with eight specific ways he could help. He never wrote back.

I earnestly needed support from SAASS because the school oversaw my PhD and my career trajectory. SAASS faculty cherished their mission of educating strategists who creatively applied airpower to achieve U.S. national interests. They taught airpower theory, strategy, international relations, and military innovation. We read case studies of disruptive military officers who took great risks and challenged conventional thinking to lead some of the greatest military transformations of the 20th century. I saw myself as living out everything SAASS had educated me to do.

Key leaders at SAASS had only one concern: that I stop pursuing frivolous distractions and focus on my PhD. Our correspondence grew tense and then adversarial.

To keep going, I needed one resource more than anything else: my own time. With the help of friends working in Air Force Headquarters, I made an unconventional ask to extend my time at Stanford, which would give me the breathing room to continue Uplift while still completing my PhD. Key stakeholders in Air Force Headquarters supported the ask, especially after the briefing to the Chief of Staff, but a SAASS administrator killed it.

Brandon was also in a precarious place with his advisor. His overcommitment to the project meant that he would now need an additional year to graduate. I felt terrible about putting him in this position.

We needed to slow down but we were trapped.

Momentum had taken over.

Our nonprofit was broke, but Brian had finished our fundraising video and the BBC story would air in a month. That media wave would be our one and only chance to fundraise and prepare for a summer demo in Turkey. If we slowed down, the organization would die.

We kept at it.

While we waited for the BBC story to go live, we fundraised across our network. It did not go well. The CEO of a drone company pledged help, then backed off after talking to his lawyers.

Prominent philanthropists expressed vague admiration but offered no support. When we sent out our first newsletter, several nonprofit leaders promptly unsubscribed. We were baffled and demoralized.

I found no meaningful support at Stanford. For all the talk about world-changing social innovation, money made Silicon Valley go round. Nobody could understand why we hadn't organized Uplift as a for-profit company. Two student groups at the Stanford Graduate School of Business developed business plans to turn Uplift into a sustainable corporation. Both ditched the mission of breaking sieges in Syria. There was no profit in serving destitute populations in war zones.

Someone suggested crowdfunding. That idea intimidated me. Crowdfunding depended on donor rewards, but we could not guarantee success. My teammates argued that our donors would understand that.

It still seemed terribly risky.

Experienced leaders tell you, "It's lonely at the top." This was definitely true during this season. I believed we were moving too fast, but I also knew my weaknesses: I avoid risks in the absence of information, rarely ask for help, and am terrible at marketing. I loathed Silicon Valley hustlers who raised millions selling pipe dreams. My style was to underpromise and overdeliver. Like many artists, I preferred to stay quiet, head down, laser-focused on craftsmanship and quality. If we did that, I thought, support would come.

That approach clearly had not worked.

The team was right; we needed to ask for help.

I agonized over the decision.

During this season I read Peter Diamandis' book *Bold*, which urges audacity at critical moments like these. Many failed entrepreneurs give up at precisely the moment they should double down.

Crowdfunding offered our best shot at reaching Turkey. So we were bold.

The team ran an amazing campaign. Our webpage told an extraordinary story. Brian's fundraising video and the BBC clip beautifully showcased our vision, capabilities, and needs.[7] We tried to excite potential donors while honestly communicating the risks and uncertainty.

We reached out to everyone we knew: Air Force leadership, State Department officials, advisors to UN Ambassador Samantha Power. One team member met Stefan de Mistura, the UN Special Representative for Syria. We spoke at humanitarian conferences in Cyprus and at MIT. We pitched to Peter Diamandis' Singularity University.

Donations arrived but we noted an alarming trend: support mostly came from family and friends. Despite the publicity wave, few outside donations poured in. The big aid organizations barely stirred. Neither did Syrians. BBC botched the Arabic version of the story, which conflated my military service with the Syria Airlift Project in a way that prompted an outcry about American imperialism.

The night before the crowdfunding campaign ended, we still needed $4,000 to reach our $40,000 goal. The crowdfunding site used an all-or-nothing model and would refund all donations unless we closed that gap by midnight. At the last minute, a relative donated $5,000. He called to say that he found our work inspiring at a time when so much about American politics left him depressed and cynical. His faith and generosity humbled me, but I felt sick with fear. I worried his faith was misplaced.

Even as the campaign was underway, I worked around the clock on approvals and logistics to recreate our Sacramento demo in Turkey. We only had a few months to prepare.

Turkey looked less and less viable. ISIS—later the Islamic State—had rampaged across Syria over the previous year, changing everything. International will to support the Syrian opposition evaporated. ISIS spread into Turkey, creating severe danger along the border. The last thing Turkey needed was a crazy fly-by-night humanitarian venture creating new risks on its soil.

Our options narrowed week by week. Our appeals to the Turkish government hit dead ends. U.S. officials expressed admiration for our work but saw no way forward.

We were raising funds for an operation that looked less and less viable. I could barely function because of the stress. I delegated almost every aspect of the crowdfunding campaign because even looking at the page made me physically ill.

I kept chanting Diamandis' mantra: Be bold. Be bold. Be bold.

We had always insisted that our planes must launch from a neighboring country like Turkey or Jordan, subject to third-party monitoring. It was the safest way to ensure that Syrians embroiled in a losing war would not repurpose our planes as weapons.

With Turkey off the table, our Syrian friends and advisors urged us to reconsider. If we could just ship the planes to Turkey or Jordan, they could transport the planes to trusted agents inside Syria and launch from there.

A viable plan came together. A friend ran a nonprofit in Jordan that taught Syrian refugees to design and build custom prosthetics. He helped us draft a proposal to stand up a drone program at his makerspace. If we offered drone training to Jordanian students, the Jordanian government—always looking to grow its private sector—might support us. Once that operation was up and running, we could also train teams who would enter Syria. A former British diplomat helped us pitch the proposal to the Jordanian government.

A crisis erupted in our team when I announced this possibility. We were reversing a well-reasoned decision, some team members said. They worried about the higher risk of weaponization. And because U.S. and Australian sanctions law prohibited the export of drones to Syria, we could be found guilty of breaking the law. We planned to seek exemptions to sanctions law, but even so, several team members resigned.

Around this time a feud erupted between two of the Syrian organizations I relied on. Even as an Arabic-speaking Middle East specialist, Syria was largely opaque to me; anything we did inside the country required putting extraordinary faith in local partners. I had no idea which organization to trust.

Summer drew closer.

Another option emerged. A month after our Refugee Empowerment Event, a terrible earthquake in Nepal drew attention to the humanitarian potential of drones. I invited Stanford's Nepali students to fly with us one day. They still had friends and family in Nepal, and I wanted to hear whether they thought these drones would add value. We had a wonderful time, and the flights went perfectly. The students saw tremendous potential for delivering water filtration systems to remote areas.

A Nepali nonprofit wanted to stand up a humanitarian drone lab in Kathmandu, and a large philanthropic organization offered Uplift a $40,000 grant to support the effort. Executing a Nepal project would detour us away from Syria, but would demonstrate our capabilities and give us practice deploying in an operational environment.

I dragged my feet on a decision.

So many variables were in play now. We continued to explore last options for Turkey, still waited on answers from Jordan, and still tried to make sense of the Syria option.

We had so little time.

As the spring quarter wound down, I discovered that I had made a catastrophic mistake. For the entire past year we had built towards a summer deployment to Turkey, so I had assumed that much of our team would be available.

I was wrong. Nearly our entire engineering team departed campus for the summer. Those who remained had a combination of vacations, research obligations, and internships. Not a single engineer would be available to travel to Jordan or Nepal in August. The consequences of having an all-volunteer team became increasingly apparent.

June arrived. We sat on $40,000 of crowdfunded donations. Friends and supporters asked about our progress. I had no idea how to keep faith with our donors.

My sense of personal failure was constant and inescapable now. I lived in perpetual exhaustion, and the simple act of checking my email hurled me into an emotional abyss. No amount of rest and recuperation could remove the weight of responsibility from my shoulders. I saw no relief on the horizon. I had never felt so hopeless.

My family felt the strain. We limited our summer vacations because I needed to be available to travel to Jordan or Nepal, possibly alone.

My health suffered. On my 35th birthday I felt a terrible rip in my lower back while water skiing. I could barely move for two weeks. My mental health plummeted. I had always been even-keeled, but could barely manage my erratic emotions now.

A deeper and more personal battle had also been unfolding. I grew up as a devout evangelical Christian, but doubts had always tormented me, and my faith had steadily unraveled over the past fifteen years. Now, with so little left, I finally acknowledged that I could no longer identify as a Christian. The grief, pain, and loss were unlike anything I had ever experienced. I had no idea who I was anymore. My gradual "coming out" devastated my family and friends. I had become a source of pain and grief to everyone I loved.

I was failing at the helm of Uplift, failing to be a good Christian and husband and father, failing to thrive as a graduate student, and failing to live up to the expectations of my faculty at SAASS and Stanford. I had burned so many bridges to follow my heart's call, and now everything was coming apart.

Still, I did not give up.

I flew at Lake Lagunita several times a week. I fought to keep my optimism, fought to motivate our remaining volunteers, fought to snatch victory from the jaws of defeat.

On July 3, 2015 we trekked out to Lake Lagunita for yet another day of battling Resistance. We launched Waliid, burdened with an unusually heavy payload. We pushed the limits, trying to obtain the payloads and ranges we would need in Syria.

The plane tilted right, plunged, and struck the ground.

We saw fire.

CRASH

I sat on a log while firemen battled the fire.

The only emotion I felt was grim and unexpected: relief.

Since spring I had felt increasingly trapped by our success. The project was surging ahead but I was breaking down. I could not work hard enough or fast enough to keep up, but if I stopped, everything would collapse.

Maybe now we would have an excuse to slow down. Maybe I could breathe again.

Throughout the summer, I had just one desire: to head off into the mountains with Wendy and the kids to heal. Between Stanford and Uplift, I had worked around the clock for more than a year. The project consumed every weekend, summer, and holiday break.

I dreamed of oblivion and found it in the roiling smoke.

The police and firemen treated our team with surprising calm. They thanked us for our professionalism and for calling in the fire, which would have grown into an uncontrollable wildfire otherwise. Stanford's Dean of Engineering, who happened to be on a walk around Lake Lagunita, also applauded our preparedness. I was satisfied that we had maintained our integrity.

After the firemen departed, Brandon and I walked through the blackened lakebed until we found the plane's wreckage: just twisted cinders from the carbon fiber wing spar and an ejected, heavily damaged battery. We discharged the battery, then gathered our media volunteers to write a press release. The Stanford Daily ran a story. Amazingly, the mainstream media did not pick it up. I emailed the Uplift team to tell them how proud I was of their professionalism in a crisis.

Stanford banned all drone flying at Lake Lagunita while the administration reviewed safety policies. Our relationship with the Stanford drone club had always been strong, but the club quickly distanced itself from us out of necessity.

Stanford directed us to stop using campus facilities because we were a distinct corporate entity. I understood but the restrictions stung; dozens of Stanford students founded startups in their dorms while leveraging Stanford assets.

We were different. Uplift was a pariah now.

My physical and mental health declined rapidly.

I spent the ensuing weeks in a daze. One morning I compulsively googled terms like "nervous breakdown" and "entrepreneur therapy" and "celebrate failure groups." I spent hours reading write-ups about failed startups.

I largely stopped working on school and Uplift. I played with my children. I talked with Wendy. We watched movies. I wrote raw emails to friends who let me vent without judgment. I talked to a friend who had been through her own nervous breakdown a few months prior. I wrote a candid Facebook message about failure, which alarmed more than a few friends. Classmates came by to check on me.

It felt good to be broken. For so long, people had expected me to be superhuman. I had wanted to scream, "I'm human! I have limits!" I had considered checking myself into the Emergency Room to show how dire my mental health was.

Now I could enjoy the freedom that came with being a complete wreck. For the first time that I could remember, expectations of me were low.

Brandon suffered similar challenges. He spent a family vacation contemplating whether he should quit. He was burned out and behind in school. His student funding was about to run out and his first baby was due in September. I knew he would have no meaningful ability to contribute after that.

For the first time, I raised the possibility of dissolving Uplift. I saw no way forward. The volunteer model had hit its limits, Brandon and I were broken, our engineering was going backwards, and we had no roadmap to achieve our goals in Syria. One day, for almost three hours, we debated quitting. Brandon could not bring himself to endorse the idea; the project meant too much to him.

I realized then that I might need to make the hardest leadership call of the entire project: the decision to dissolve. Nobody else would make that call.

I might need to kill Uplift to protect my volunteers from themselves.

Brandon convinced me to stick with it a little longer. He suggested we scale back our ambitions. We were putting way too much pressure on ourselves.

I called Nepal and our donor organization to cancel the Nepal project. Each call lasted less than five minutes. It was stunning how fast we could dismantle months of work.

We gathered the engineering team to study the wreckage and data logs. We theorized about why the aircraft had rolled inexplicably towards the ground. We debated what punctured the highly flammable Lithium Polymer batteries. We improved the aircraft design.

We found an RC flying field in Santa Cruz, located between a river and irrigated farmland. The drive was an hour and a half each way but at least it wouldn't burn. One Saturday a volunteer and I made the long drive down. The club welcomed us with enthusiasm. The club president showed us around and took photos of our operation for his club newspaper.

Our flights went poorly. We flew three times, but the takeoffs felt erratic and unstable. Waliid seemed underpowered and we nearly crashed. The plane had flown so well for months. Now it was dangerous and unpredictable, like an unbroken horse. We had no idea why, and went home embarrassed and demoralized.

A drone training program in Jordan was our last, desperate gamble for a success. It was late July now and the Jordanian government still had not approved the plan. We would need to order all the hardware from China, which could take weeks to arrive. That left a razor-thin margin of time for us to fly to Jordan and run the program before the fall quarter started.

The proposal called for using quadcopters, not fixed-wing planes like Uplift usually flew. I had never even built or flown a quadcopter before. I worked like a maniac to prepare. I researched kits, overnighted the most promising one, built it the following evening, and test flew it in the morning. I maintained an extreme work pace out of necessity. I largely worked alone.

When we still didn't have Jordanian approval two weeks later, I finally pulled the plug.

Summer was over.

We had no successes to show our donors, whose contributions still sat in our checking account. We could not even replicate our success five months earlier.

We made one more trip to the Santa Cruz RC field. The engineers had tweaked Waliid's center of gravity, which we thought might help the controllability issues.

Word about our project had spread, and a crowd gathered to watch. I had never felt so much pressure around a single flight. This felt like a make-or-break moment.

The bungee launcher fired. The plane soared into the air. The crowd gasped in approval. And then it all went wrong. I could barely control the plane. It stalled repeatedly. When I brought it back around towards the field, it careened wildly and stalled overhead, sending club members scrambling. I had to make three go-arounds before landing, and then the plane stalled during the flare, cartwheeled off the runway, and smashed its tail. One bystander cursed as we nearly destroyed his parked plane.

We gathered our things, cheeks burning, not making eye contact with anyone. I fled to my car. My volunteer looked to me for guidance. I sat in silence for a long time, shaking, letting the humiliation wash over me.

We had come so far, but a year and a half into this, we were still crashing planes regularly. I felt like I had during those first months in Alabama, when every flight was a wild gamble, only now the planes were bigger and heavier and more dangerous.

We were failing again.

Another accident was inevitable.

We could have jumped right back into engineering. We had probably moved the center of gravity too far aft, which destabilized the plane. We later discovered that a parameter error had capped the motor power output at a fraction of its capability. We also discovered that the rudder had somehow been trimmed far out of alignment, which contributed to a nasty rolling tendency. Our team could fix these problems.

However, these technical challenges were only symptoms of deeper organizational problems. We were not idiots; we were Stanford engineers who had been at this for a very long time, and had access to some of the best talent in the drone industry. However, we were building an incredibly complex paradigm with emerging technology using overworked volunteers. We could not do proper systems engineering, testing, or quality assurance. Our processes were immature. Glitches appeared as fast as we could squash them.

Brandon and I had worked ourselves to death preparing for this single fly day. How would we possibly keep this up, with school starting and Brandon's baby on the way?

I knew the answer: we couldn't.

I gave the order to dissolve Uplift Aeronautics.

I thought I was being heroic by making a tough, necessary call. We did our team no favors by dragging out an inevitable decision, expending more resources, and risking another accident. Better to quit now, on our terms, before school started. We could all get on with our lives. I could tackle the second year of my PhD studies unencumbered, and Brandon could welcome his new baby with undivided attention.

I misjudged. Uplift's board responded with consternation when I emailed the dissolution notice without consulting them first. I did not have the authority to dissolve the organization, they correctly noted. We were incorporated now, with a board of directors that provided governance. Most of the board did not want to quit. Brandon asked me if I would have made the same decision if Waliid's flight that week was a spectacular success.

I had reached my lowest point in the project. My leadership had become increasingly erratic. My team was losing faith in my judgment. I felt trapped by forces much larger than myself.

The team urged me to slow down and take a deep breath. We would clearly not achieve our summer goals, but we had always said that we were playing the long game. We needed to fundamentally revisit the business model and timeline and cage expectations accordingly. Our donors would understand.

Family and friends provided a consistent message: they still believed in Uplift Aeronautics and the Syria Airlift Project. They believed in me. They hoped we would continue. Their support at this dark time meant the world to me, but I knew they were the wrong people to assess decisions about the future of Uplift Aeronautics. They knew nothing of the organizational problems, the engineering challenges, the policy blockers, and the incredible personal stress we suffered.

I still felt strongly that we needed to dissolve. Failing to do so now would only prolong the agony, and we would lose the initiative. However, the board was right; I could not make this decision alone. If the team felt this strongly, I owed it to them to respect their views.

We agreed to keep Uplift Aeronautics open until the end of the calendar year. If we did not find a way forward by then, we would dissolve.

I awkwardly retracted my dissolution notice. We explained the situation to our donors and offered to refund their donations. Only one donor took us up on that offer, and a few wrote back to applaud our integrity and grit.

The immediate pressure was off.

Still, I had never felt so trapped.

EMBERS

My second year at Stanford began. I needed to deliver a major field paper in the spring, which necessitated shifting my time and energy to research, but the shadow of Uplift Aeronautics hung over me.

A sense of personal failure pervaded my life. Blows kept coming.

None of my research proposals gained any traction. Professor feedback could be ruthless, and I returned to the drawing board again and again. I still had not achieved meaningful relationships with any faculty members.

I could not shake my reputation as a problem child. The SAASS administrator who had so vehemently opposed my work for Uplift wrote an e-mail to two Colonels in my chain of command, warning them of my proclivity to distraction while at Stanford. I was furious and hurt. I had aced my comprehensive exams a semester early, achieved A's or A-'s in all my courses despite overloading on credits, and done an incredible amount of foundational work for my dissertation. I had yet to drop a ball.

If I watched TV or played golf instead of running a startup, nobody would have batted an eye.

Uplift was adrift. We no longer had a strategy or unifying goals. As soon as we made the decision to keep Uplift open, most of the team got busy with school and life and disappeared.

We scaled back our ambitions. We focused on developing building blocks that our cargo delivery paradigm would need, like a new ground control station and customized drone firmware. However, we had no strategy for integrating these building blocks into a real capability.

In December a new bombshell dropped: my Stanford faculty sent me a student progress review letter. They expressed concern that my extracurricular activities were jeopardizing my ability to complete my PhD. Their loss of faith devastated me.

I had coffee with a mentor named Kevin who had spent his career in startups and seen everything under the sun. I was a mess. Kevin listened patiently and then gave me the advice I needed to hear: it is okay to walk away. The world will keep turning. All this innovation stuff will be waiting for you later.

In the morning I told Jessie that I intended to resign from Uplift. She knew how much I had endured, and supported my decision. I notified the board. I had never asked anything of them before, but now I asked that they let me depart in peace. I also asked them to fulfill their responsibilities as board members in determining Uplift's future.

With that one email, I ended a year and a half of effort.

I would like to report an immediate process of healing.

What began instead were two years in the wilderness.

My resignation did not bring the closure I craved. It brought no fanfare, no emotional farewell, and no reminiscing on better times. I felt like an exile walking out of his village for the last time into the desert beyond.

I still felt compelled to tidy up loose ends. When the board dissolved Uplift Aeronautics a few weeks later, I drafted a letter to our donors. I worked with Jessie to donate our remaining funds to charities that supported Syrian refugees.

Any time a new siege began in Syria, humanitarian organizations reached out to me. They seemed put off when I declined to help. Every new inquiry sent me into an emotional tailspin.

My renewed focus on academia was hardly smooth.

Graduate school can wreak havoc on one's mental health in the best of times, but my devastating sense of personal failure compounded my experience. My relationships with professors at both Stanford and SAASS remained strained. I felt like a constant source of disappointment.

I spent hours alone in my head each day, working on my research in coffee shops around Stanford's park-like campus. It felt good to relax into that state of deep focus called *flow*, and give myself without abandon to my research.

As the weeks passed, however, these hours felt increasingly ominous. My spring deadline was approaching but none of my work was coming together. I spent weeks on a paper that my advisor dismissed with a brief email. He made no suggestion of reframing, editing, or salvaging.

I started over on a new paper more in line with his expectations. It was a disaster. My messy, ambiguous data did not yield useful findings. When I presented an early draft, my critique group sat in silent pity, contemplating how to salvage something. The meeting ended with vague encouragements to keep at it.

Helplessness might be the most stressful human emotion. That is the story of graduate school for many people: a black curtain of helplessness spread over years of your life. You toil for days and weeks and months, fighting your inner demons, battling Resistance, trying to claw something together that isn't terrible. Then you present your work to a single fallible human being who is busy and distracted and has a hundred other responsibilities. This individual holds the keys to your academic success and possibly your entire career. Earning that individual's approval becomes your entire universe.

Nothing is ever quite good enough.

You walk away devastated. Then you have to try again.

Meanwhile, my friends seemed to be reaching the peak of professional success. Witnessing their achievements felt devastating. Social media was a minefield. Anytime a friend announced the publication of a new academic article, I plunged into an abyss of self-loathing. When my former volunteers landed speaking gigs at conferences, I cheered them on but also felt resentment.

At Stanford I was surrounded by successful, wealthy, beautiful people who showed no evidence of mental health struggles. Wendy and I developed a private joke. When she informed me that our next-door neighbor was an Olympic runner, I said, *Of course she is.* Her new buddy in the cycling club is a Vice President of a Fortune 100 company? *Of course he is.* Our friend is launching a venture fund to help Haitian entrepreneurs rebuild their devastated country? *Of course he is.*

We used this joke weekly.

Then there was me: languishing alone amidst my rejected papers, never good enough for my faculty, with SAASS shining its search light on me to ensure I wasn't letting them down again.

My religious deconstruction continued to be a source of shame and grief. Wendy and I spent many hours talking through the uncertain implications for our marriage, which was deeply rooted in Christianity. We had no idea what to tell our children. Close friends regarded my journey as a tragedy. I kept my religious views secret from almost everyone else. I struggled to find community.

My health problems continued. My back injury had never fully healed, and one evening while running I felt an excruciating pain in my right knee. I had injured my IT band, likely a side effect of my back problems. Weeks of rest did nothing to heal the injury.

I had always been in excellent health. Never before had my body been unable to perform a basic function. I had never felt so weak.

As I approached my third and final year, I considered my future after Stanford. The same SAASS administrator who had opposed my work on the Syria Airlift Project was equally adamant that I become a squadron commander. This was the normal progression for a high-performing Air Force officer, but I did not want a conventional Air Force career. I had spent my life developing a highly specialized skill set. I could do things that nobody else in the Air Force could, if I just had the chance.

My choices were constrained by a bureaucratic personnel system that centrally manages the careers of the entire Air Force. I searched and searched for opportunities that would utilize my skills. The Secretary of Defense launched a new Defense Innovation Unit: Experimental (DIUx) in Silicon Valley, which seemed perfect, but my inquiries went unanswered. In the end, I found no support for an alternative assignment. I dutifully applied for the squadron command I did not want. The board passed me over.

This was not fatal, as I would have been eligible to try again later, but it felt like a further unraveling. My leadership had opposed my greatest professional contribution to the Air Force. They kept pushing me along a track I never wanted, and now that track led into an uncertain wilderness. I had no idea what to do next.

I felt like I had fallen through the cracks of the world. I had voluntarily walked away from the Air Force's fast track. My Stanford and SAASS faculty saw me as a struggling student. The Air Force's innovation communities showed no interest in me. The Air Force personnel system saw me only as a pilot who had lost his way.

I drifted on, a ship dead in the water, just trying to stay afloat.

I kept up my research and writing. I wrote for hours and hours every morning, but by afternoon most days I felt despondent. I learned through experience when it was time to close the laptop and go play with my kids.

Slowly, I found glimmers of hope.

My research yielded a breakthrough discovery at the 11th hour. The paper quickly wrote itself. My advisor praised the work. I was finally building relationships with other professors and pulling together a dissertation committee.

One paper down.

Three papers would count as a complete dissertation.

I signed up for a swimming class. A physical therapist successfully treated my IT band injury, and within a month I was able to run short distances again. In the spring, around the time I submitted my research paper, I ran my first triathlon.

I was slowly getting strong again.

Every time I thought life had turned a corner, another blow fell.

That summer I got scabies. Every morning in the predawn hours, I awoke to sharp nipping between my fingers and around my crotch. I could not hug my wife or children for months. Dermatologists repeatedly misdiagnosed me. The condition was humiliating and awkward. I had always thought scabies was an STD so wondered if people assumed I was being unfaithful to Wendy.

By fall I was healthy again and determined to make the school year a success. I joined the Stanford triathlon team, began training daily, and did a second triathlon in October. I felt fantastic.

My advisor seemed happy with my research progress.

In November, while on a much-needed Disneyland vacation with my family, I received a phone call from the graduate student advisor. She had just learned that my advisor was leaving the country for the rest of the year. He had not told anybody.

Time stopped.

I could barely breathe.

How had I not known this?

Vacation ruined, I spent the rest of the day trying to gather information. My advisor urged me not to worry. He said I could defend in January before he left, months earlier than planned. His confidence stunned me, especially since I had turned in only a third of a dissertation.

We met after my vacation to discuss my work. That meeting unraveled every gain I had made in the past year.

This was the first time he had really sat down to look at the totality of my work. He hated it. He got visibly agitated as he critiqued a paper I was writing for another professor. "This is nowhere near the quality of what I would sign off in a dissertation," he said. Nor did he like the third paper, which was based on an outline we had developed together a few months prior.

With six months left to graduate, my entire dissertation plan was in flames.

I quit the triathlon team. My physical health plummeted.

I began having chronic nightmares. In one dream I became lost in a wilderness and screamed at the top of my lungs for help. In another dream I broke down and sobbed in my advisor's office.

There was no escape.

I had to work through the failure.
There was no other way.

One ray of light broke through. I had spent months trying to obtain an assignment at DIUx, to no avail. Now, out of nowhere, I received an e-mail from an Air Force officer at DIUx named Lieutenant Colonel David "Mudd" Willard who had encountered my work with drones. The Islamic State was building a drone air force to rain down grenades on U.S. and allied troops in Iraq and Syria, and DoD was scrambling to respond.

Mudd invited me to speak at DIUx. I owned most of the drones the Islamic State used, so carted them in for a show-and-tell session. After my talk, one of DIUx's partners—the former Director of Operations for Google X, Google's fabled moonshot division—told me I was hired.

I could not believe this abrupt reversal of fortune. After two and a half years of suffering in the wilderness, I had *finally* found a place that valued and appreciated what I could bring. Taking the job would mean sacrifices. I would never fly again, would take a significant pay cut, and would probably not get promoted again, but I could use my unique skills to do work I believed in.

Even as I struggled to finish my dissertation, I began attending meetings at DIUx. We listened to company pitches for drone and counter-drone technology. I had more technical expertise than anybody in the room. My colleagues valued and respected me. I could have wept with gratitude at finding a place where I belonged.

Every success proved to be fleeting.

It turned out that the former Director of Operations for Google X had overstepped by promising to hire me. I learned later that he had no authority to do so. In fact, nobody did.

Every single person in DoD had to fit into positions called

"billets", which are managed by vast bureaucracies that would put Soviet economic planners to shame. Because pilots are so rare and valuable, obtaining new pilot billets is almost impossible. DIUx had no way to hire me.

The Air Force had already turned off my other assignment options. I had nowhere else to go.

Everyone agreed that I belonged at DIUx. DIUx's leadership and general officers from multiple Air Force headquarters got involved. Nobody could solve the puzzle. Their efforts gradually flagged. Email threads died off.

My family and I were under severe stress. We had no idea what would happen next, where we would be living in three months, or what plans we should make for our kids' school.

The Air Force had no place for me anymore.

I was back in the wilderness.

I kept at my dissertation every day.

I met with any faculty member who would see me. I brought outlines and proposals. I went to student critique groups. I churned through draft after draft, molding raw material, trying to shape it into something tolerable. I worked right through Christmas break. My advisor was no doubt as exhausted as I was.

In January I finished my second major section and wasted no time starting the third. In these final months I became laser-focused, writing for hours every morning and then plowing through musty books in the Stanford library in the afternoons. I felt like one of those railroad workers in old movie clips, furiously laying track as the train chugs along behind.

In May I defended.

I only invited my wife and a few close friends. I could not bear the shame of failing in front of a large group.

After my presentation, my advisor's first question was, "What are your odds of getting a fourth year?"

After a lengthy discussion, my committee dismissed me so they could deliberate.

Eventually my advisor entered the room where I waited. He extended a hand and said, "Congratulations, Dr. Jacobsen."

I was finally emerging from the wilderness.

A supportive SAASS professor suggested a creative solution to my billet problem. SAASS owned unfilled billets for pilots. The school could make me a SAASS professor but remotely assign me to DIUx. After my years of fraught relations with the school, this breathtaking gift changed everything. *This* was the unconventional, disruptive support I had longed for. My SAASS family enabled me to do something novel and important for the Air Force, something that only I could do.

Ideas swirled in my mind.

I knew what I wanted to tackle next.

RENEWAL

Shortly after I defended my dissertation, I pitched a new venture to DIUx leadership: a drone "red team" called Rogue Squadron. We would build an insurgent drone air force to help DoD anticipate and respond to emerging drone threats.

My cofounder was Navy Lieutenant Ryan Beall, a helicopter pilot just finishing his master's degree at Naval Postgraduate School and transitioning into DIUx. Ryan had spent much of his career designing and building drones and related hardware.

The proposal raised skeptical eyebrows, but DIUx's leadership embraced a culture of experimentation. They gave me a green light and $5,000. A month later, they upped that to $25,000. By the end of that first summer, our projects were gaining traction. The Secretary of Defense visited DIUx in August, saw what Rogue Squadron was developing, and personally directed us to scale a project. Overnight, our budget grew into the millions, which allowed us to build a team of full-time software developers and drone technicians.

Rogue Squadron was real.

I was back in the saddle.

Founding Rogue Squadron gave me something exceptional: a second chance.

I effectively became the founder and CEO of another drone startup with a compelling mission. This time we were not volunteers; we were paid professionals. We had resources. Although we were insurgents within the vast bureaucracy of the Department of Defense, we found institutional support and allies.

Over the next two years, Rogue Squadron arguably became the most effective small drone team in the United States government. We found, courted, and hired some of the top drone hackers in the world. We fielded six apps to more than 200 organizations across the Department of Defense, other federal agencies, and allied countries. Our demand curve was literally exponential.

We had a novel business model of working directly for warfighters, bypassing most intermediate headquarters. We leveraged best practices from the private sector like agile development and DevOps—which meant we could operate at breathtaking speed. In one case we received a call for help from U.S. troops in Syria and delivered new software capability in less than two hours.

Special Operations Forces soldiers told us our capabilities saved lives. Our software helped government agencies fight wildfires, rescue a hiker stranded in a Hawaiian lava field, and defeat improvised explosive devices in the Middle East. We built and scaled a drone detection system across multiple countries. We helped interdict drone-enabled drug smuggling, and helped architect a strategy to revitalize the American drone industry and break an emerging monopoly by a single foreign company.

None of this came easy.

Our business model directly challenged entrenched interests. Bureaucrats continually tried to undermine us. A government program manager reverse-engineered our code and gave it to his favorite vendor. Risk-averse staffers tried to shut down our efforts, stall our projects, and overclassify our work. Despite the large number of U.S. soldiers using our capabilities, we lacked institutional support from key defense leaders. Funding vanished without explanation. We struggled to get the needed manpower and partnerships.

Life as an insurgent can be exhilarating, but you are always one mistake away from annihilation.

The lessons from Uplift proved to be invaluable.

Ryan's and my expertise with small drones became the foundation of Rogue Squadron's capabilities. From a technical point of view, covertly delivering humanitarian packages in war zones was almost identical to dropping munitions. Ryan and I knew exactly how insurgents would build, train, and utilize drone air forces, which gave us intuitions about how to outwit them.

I also knew how to build and lead a dynamic organization. Most days I acted swiftly, confidently, and decisively. Uncertainty did not faze me. I had an intuitive sense for how to bootstrap the team and achieve increasingly ambitious milestones. We avoided traps and land mines.

Most importantly, I knew how to manage myself.

Rising each day to fight new battles was exhausting, but I paced myself and urged my teammates to do the same. I frequently withdrew into my journal, meditation, and physical exercise. I was proud of our successes but not attached to them. I knew how quickly our fortunes could change. I was relentlessly determined to make Rogue Squadron a success but also prepared for its failure.

I loved my guys and what they were achieving.

I was not always happy, but Rogue Squadron gave me purpose.

Just as failure had seemed to infect every part of my life, so did this sense of renewal.

SAASS had a new Commandant who loved Rogue Squadron. He flew out to see our lab firsthand and returned home ecstatic. Later, he asked me to guest-teach a three-week SAASS course on military innovation. I did, and discovered that this arrangement offered the perfect balance of my entrepreneurial and academic interests.

The next year, he appointed me to be Course Director. I made bold changes, and the new course received rave reviews.

After all my struggles at Stanford, I had finally found my place in academia.

The fear and shame surrounding my faith journey gradually subsided. I found a new sense of peace, as I embraced my emerging identity. I liked who I was now. After more than a decade of debilitating cognitive dissonance, I was finally living out an authentic identity. I could stand confidently on my beliefs.

My interactions with others became deeper, more authentic, and more wholehearted. It took time to process my journey with my loved ones, but they gradually realized that I was still the same person. Some relationships faded but others deepened. New friends entered my life.

I retained the best elements of my Christian upbringing, like a worldview of forgiveness, grace, and radical love. I do not believe in God most days, but I think I am a better Christian than I ever was before.

At some point, I was able to look back and see that my season of failure was largely behind me. I knew that failure would come for me again, as it always does. However, I no longer feared failure and felt able to rest in the quiet joys of this new season.

In the desolate weeks after the Stanford fire, I had started writing as a means of taming my anxiety. One day, sitting in a Palo Alto Starbucks, I spent hours laboring at my academic research. Nothing came. As I stared at the blinking cursor, cold talons squeezed my chest. Waves of self-doubt rolled over me, with frightening and escalating intensity.

I closed my laptop and tried to read instead.

No luck. I was trapped in my own mind.

Eventually, in desperation, I opened my laptop, started a new file, and unleashed a raw, brutal stream of consciousness onto the page. It brought a strange sense of relief. In the months that followed, I continued to write as a form of catharsis. During each session I reflected on some new aspect of my own experience. In doing so, I often arrived at new insights.

As time went by and the hurts ebbed, I began to write about the lessons learned, my aspirations, and my steps towards growth and new life. I only wrote intermittently, but the journal was always there, always calling me towards deeper explorations.

As these writings accumulated, I saw the potential for turning them into a book, a kind of guided tour through failure and its aftermath. I reshaped material, sculpting my first suggestive impressions into meaningful wholes.

Trying to pin down a narrative arc was darkly comic because my life kept making radical swings between success and failure.

When I resigned from Uplift, I wrote about my hope of building a new identity as a scholar. When my dissertation went off the rails, I emphasized the repeated cycle of failure and success. Getting hired at DIUx made me hopeful again, and the book ended on a triumphant note. Six months later, when it looked like my DIUx assignment would fall through, I wrote about looking beyond success and failure and instead accepting the journey through both.

After I founded Rogue Squadron, I wondered if I was qualified to write about failure anymore. After all, I was succeeding again.

Then more setbacks came.

I felt exhausted, like a day trader trying to time the market.

I just needed to finish the damn book.

It is to these writings that we turn now. All of us who have reached our breaking points have a unique story to tell, but these stories often follow similar arcs. In the next four parts of the book, we will walk this inner journey together—through failure, aftermath, healing, and renewal. I mostly write in the second person, but these are my deepest meditations on what I personally experienced.

It is not an easy journey. We will eat glass together, but we will find new life along the way.

PART TWO

FAILING

THE FIRST STEP

And now we return to the beginning.

The wheels are coming off. The critics hate the thing you have poured your heart and soul into for the past two years. You are in a death spiral of complexity. You are hemorrhaging cash and bankruptcy looks imminent. The board has lost confidence in you. Your screenplay is a disaster. It looks like your injury will never fully heal. Awareness dawns that your relationship might really be over.

For me, it was looking out over the blackened ruin of Lake Lagunita, knowing in my gut that we were finished—but also knowing that I was still at the helm, psychologically shattered, with months of excruciating leadership challenges ahead.

Together we stand at the brink, looking out over this vista of failure. It stretches farther than we can see.

The only way across is straight through.

They say the journey of a thousand miles begins with the first step.

So let's close our eyes.

Take a breath.

We will make it through. I promise.

Let's step.

VERTIGO

Failure throws your well-ordered universe into turmoil.

Everything you thought you knew is suddenly proved wrong. You have read all the motivational books, watched all the TED talks, and studied the biographies of renegade entrepreneurs like Steve Jobs and Elon Musk. You know all about daring greatly, being a disruptive innovator, making moonshots, and possessing grit. Friends come to you for advice. You could make a fortune as a life coach, if you wished. Maybe you already are.

Suddenly none of it works.

Every pilot has experienced a phenomenon called spatial disorientation. You are cruising straight and level through the clouds, unable to see the ground, when all of a sudden, your body is absolutely convinced that you are in a steep turn. Pilots have corkscrewed themselves right into the ground, trying to level out of turns that never existed.

Spatial disorientation terrifies you because your most basic physical instincts betray you. Your universe bends sideways and spins. All you can do is hang on, sweating, clinging to the few reliable indicators on your instrument panel, until your scrambled sensory system reboots and the universe rights itself.

Failure hits the same way. It's pure vertigo. And there are no instruments.

Sustained failure is so disorienting because the mythology of entrepreneurship has no place for it.

We need the mythology because, as we discussed in the Introduction, entrepreneurship is so miserably hard. Nobody would do it otherwise.

Elon Musk famously said, "Being an entrepreneur is like eating glass and staring into the abyss of death." We chuckle at that. We slap it on motivational posters.

I don't think Elon was being amusing. I suspect he spoke those words with the thousand-yard stare of a war veteran. This is a man who nearly presided over the bankruptcy of two world-changing companies while undergoing a painful divorce and parenting two children.

Elon said that a failed venture activates the same portions of the brain as physical death. I do not think he researched the neuroscience of failure out of mere curiosity. He sought to understand a personal, intimate, and visceral experience. Such suffering is the price of admission for trying great things.

By one estimate, 75% of venture-backed startups fail to return their investors' capital. I suspect the success rates of diets, first novels, and marathon training programs is not significantly higher. With these odds, it takes a special kind of insanity to pursue an ambitious dream.

And yet for human progress to occur, we have to try. We need that messy churn of entrepreneurial activity for the winning ideas to emerge. That means we need entrepreneurs, and we must equip them for battles that will test them to the core.

So we create myths. We infuse this perilous journey with glory and hope. The purveyors of our modern myths are not so different from medieval popes calling Europe's young men to glory and eternal salvation on crusade.

Today our myths take new forms: the self-help and business

shelves at Barnes and Noble, TED talks, the Ponzi scheme of entrepreneurial life coaches teaching you how to earn passive income from blogs about entrepreneurial life coaching.

In good American fashion, we have invented and commercialized an entire industry around the mythology that enables and sustains brave new ventures.

It sells. Demand is endless.

When you are making forward progress, entrepreneurial mythology seems to provide sure guidance. You apply lean startup principles and build minimum viable products. You ideate and iterate. You hire slowly and fire quickly. You take audacious risks. You are exhausted and stressed and face continuous setbacks, but you know to expect this. You have *grit*. You won't give up because you are a *badass*.

Then failure pushes you over the edge.

You are in darkness unlike anything you have encountered in podcasts or websites. The blows come faster than you ever imagined possible. You know you should pick yourself up off the mat, raise your gloves, and fight another round, but at some point, you *can't*.

Nothing has prepared you for this. You now face decisions that violate all that sunny wisdom. Instead of being *bold*, you scale back. Instead of being *resilient*, you drink. You cannot *iterate* because you cannot burn scarce cash on another failed prototype. You cannot *fail fast, fail often, and fail forward* because it will take months to clean up the fallout from your latest disaster. You need to explain to your Kickstarter funders why you won't deliver their products, tell your VCs they've lost their money, or tell your partner that you've been fired. The criminal investigation into your company's misconduct will take years, and the press is camped on your lawn. That, and you are so fucked up that you can barely get out of bed.

When I reached this point, all those bestsellers made me want to vomit. I felt anger towards those authors, podcasters, and mentors who led me to this place. My eyes scanned my bookshelf in despair. *This* was the real deal; *this* was the crucible of leadership. Nothing in my education or experience had prepared me for it.

I felt like Jesus, alone, sweating blood in the garden.

IDEAS

The mythology of entrepreneurship rests on an implicit assumption: *all new ideas possess unrecognized brilliance.* If you can stick with your idea long enough, your time will come.

When you are failing, you must confront the awful possibility that this is not actually true.

In the beginning, the idea feels so right. A degree to complete. A race to run. A heart to woo. A company to found. Humanitarian aid to deliver in war-torn Syria.

Passion infuses you with superhuman energy. You do the hard work of translating that intangible dream into something real. You design, iterate, and pivot. You build and field your minimum viable product. You run 3k, then 5k, then 7k. One chapter of your novel turns into two and then three. Your romance blossoms.

A community forms around your idea. Family and friends cheer you on—some of them, anyway. Allies rally to your side. Devoted fans love your idea, celebrate your progress, and delight in sharing your journey. You bask in that affirmation for days. Every pledge of support confirms your instinct that you are onto something.

Then you hit the wall.

Your advisor hates your dissertation proposal. You get a stress fracture. Your partner turns abusive. Customers fail to materialize. Colleagues ridicule your new proposal.

Entrepreneurial mythology is there for you. You settle in with a cup of coffee and your list of favorite inspirational quotes. Thomas Edison tells you, "Nearly every man who develops an idea works it up to the point where it looks impossible, and then he gets discouraged. That's not the place to become discouraged." Edison has the street cred to say that; he's the guy who found ten thousand ways to make light bulbs that don't work.

You add a little Albert Einstein to the cocktail: "If at first the idea is not absurd, then there is no hope for it."

You stir in some Mark Twain for good measure: "The man with a new idea is a crank—until the idea succeeds."

You add a dash of Jeff Bezos: "Invention requires a long-term willingness to be misunderstood."

These quotes are witty, inspiring, and absolutely true. We canonize them in the mythology for good reason. Most successful innovations begin this way. So do most athletic achievements, successful relationships, or completed self-improvement programs. Any new idea looks crazy until it doesn't. You need faith, commitment, and a thick skin.

However, this inspirational framing overlooks one inconvenient fact: many ideas are not brilliant. Many ideas are mediocre. Some ideas are terrible, and the only humane thing is to let them die.

Of course, few innovators get the idea right the first time. That is why we promote rapid learning and iteration as best practices. Books like *The Lean Startup* urge entrepreneurs to treat every business plan as a hypothesis, which they should test as early as possible with real customers. Founders should expect to pivot again and again. They should never stop learning, even if they preside over a corporate empire.

Some ideas just need time to develop. Many entrepreneurs rush ahead of technology. The market delivered generations of lousy, overpriced, hard-to-use Portable Digital Assistants before the iPhone got it right. Early designers had the right idea but lacked the tools to execute properly.

Other entrepreneurs have the technology but get ahead of the market. I have spent much of my career trying to push innovative technology through Department of Defense bureaucracies designed before my parents were born. It doesn't matter how stellar a new capability is if I have to wait for a generation of career bureaucrats to retire before an idea can bloom.

Some flawed ideas lead us toward promising adjacent opportunities. Maybe our five-star Pet Yoga studio did not drum up the customer enthusiasm we expected but we discovered an unmet need for urban pet-setting. A slight pivot and business is humming.

Sticking with ideas is important. We should not give up too early.

Relationships are not so different. Everyone has their quirks, and a successful dating relationship requires patience and forgiveness. Successful marriages are built on years of commitment through good times and bad. You must forgive, endure, and bear with each other.

So with any other venture in life. Almost any creative work feels like a dumpster fire until it comes into focus. While writing my dissertation, I kept this Stephen King quote on my desktop:

> Stopping a piece of work just because it's hard either emotionally or imaginatively is a bad idea. Sometimes you have to go on when you don't feel like it and sometimes you're doing good work when it feels like all you're managing to do is shovel shit from a sitting position.

I read that quote every day. It is very, very hard to make an idea shine. The mythology exists for a reason.

But some ideas never get there.

Most businesses fail because they do not offer sufficient value to customers. No matter how brilliant an entrepreneur found his or her value proposition, customers disagreed.

If you are an entrepreneur, you must continually ask hard questions. Are you facing mere bumps in the road, or do these problems indicate a fatal weakness? How hard should you press in the face of criticism and naysaying? At what point should you be concerned?

You must ask similar questions in your relationships. Despite your desire to see the best in your partner, the questions can pile up: are these ordinary troubles like any couple endures, or are these worse? Are we actually a terrible match?

When do you admit that you were woefully unequipped for your expedition up Mt. Everest and that continuing will probably kill you? When do you accept that this particular university or degree program was a mistake, or that you are ill-suited for your new job?

Do you need dogged persistence, or do you need to get your goddamn life back?

I still do not know if the Syria Airlift Project was a brilliant idea or a dreadful one.

Using swarms of drones to break sieges in a conflict zone was outrageous. Our effort could have failed in so many ways, and mistakes might cost lives.

We responsibly challenged our own thinking. We kept a running list of all the ways the project could go wrong. If insurgents or terrorists stole the planes, they could be repurposed as weapons. The Syrian regime or terrorist groups could kidnap or kill our launch crews. The regime might retaliate against our effort by closing off other aid channels. A drone might collide with a civilian airliner. Armed groups could target aid recipients. In two years of giving talks, nobody ever suggested a risk we had not already considered. These considerations guided our work.

We certainly had critics who hated the idea. You will aid and abet terrorists, they said. You will proliferate a technology that will kill Americans. Your tiny toy packages do not justify the risks.

Maybe the critics were right.

In those moments of doubt, I reminded myself of our core vision: *we are trying to create a world in which no parent has to watch their child die because starvation is being used as a weapon.* Ending the use of starvation as a weapon is a good idea, even if the details are negotiable.

We kept faith with that idea.

However, once we started to rack up failures, we had to examine ourselves in the mirror. We only found a few allies willing to help us execute. Every crash carried risks of damage, injury, or even death. Our all-volunteer model proved to be unsustainable. Critical stakeholders never aligned behind our vision. Every one of these setbacks indicated a severe problem.

I agonized over the implications.

At some point, you have to ask when to let an idea go.

You have spent so long on your project, and invested so much, that you are the last person in the world who can objectively assess its merits. Self-doubt eats you alive. Even as you heroically battle Resistance to see your idea through, you begin to lose faith. And without that faith, fighting each day's battles becomes increasingly difficult.

That leads to the hardest decision of all: when to quit.

QUITTING

The foundation of entrepreneurial mythology is *grit*. Grit gives you the courage to begin an extraordinary venture when all odds are against you. Grit allows you to persevere when you are cold, alone, friendless, indebted, broken, or blocked. Grit ensures you return to your desk, workbench, or gym after every new failure.

Grit is the single characteristic that unites successful entrepreneurs throughout history. It carries university students through to graduation, a couple through fifty years of marriage, or an aspiring author onto the New York Times bestseller list. Grit separates the winners from the losers.

Aspiring entrepreneurs tremble reverently before the concept of grit. We read books about how to obtain it. We pay big bucks to listen to those gritty stalwarts who came before us, hoping just a little of their grit will rub off on us.

Like most things in the mythology, the concept is largely true. You do need grit to succeed at hard ventures. You need grit to ride out what Scott Weiss calls "WFIO" moments: *we're fucked, it's over*.[8] You need grit to turn around your failing company, save your dying marriage, finish your first marathon, or write your novel.

But this myth of grit has a dark side.

Sometimes grit is not enough. Sometimes WFIO is not just a bump along the road. Sometimes you really are fucked.

It is true that many entrepreneurs fail because of insufficient grit. Setbacks always come fast and furious when you try hard things, and many people cannot hang. No insurmountable obstacle stands in their way, but they deplete their strength and tap out when a stronger soul might have persevered.

However, some obstacles really are insurmountable. The opportunity costs might become so high that continuing makes no sense. Sometimes calling it a day is your best possible option, and persevering is nothing more than irrational obstinacy. When one line of attack has clearly failed, you might need to regroup, regather your strength, and find a new way forward.

The problem is that you rarely know which way to tilt. All you have is your educated judgment, and when you are in the midst of failure, faith in your own judgment is the first thing to go.

Are you really up against an insurmountable obstacle? Or do you lack grit?

I would like to think we showed grit with the Syria Airlift Project. We overcame hundreds of obstacles, many of which demanded every last ounce of strength we possessed. We coped with dozens of crashes. We overcame political battles and fierce resistance. Even after the Stanford fire, we kept going. After many exhausting and frustrating days, I slipped away to reflect on the latest setback, gather my strength, and find a new way forward.

However, as time went by and the failures compounded, continuing looked more like stubbornness than valor.

I agonized over grit. We had clearly reached another WFIO moment; was it the kind of WFIO moment you pushed through or the kind that killed you?

By the end, I seethed when supporters urged us to keep going and bought me fresh copies of *Bold*. I had no idea how the hell we were supposed to double down, with the organization burning down around us.

I did not need encouragement to be bold; I needed help.

In the end, we quit.

It was the only possible decision, and yet all that motivational literature still taunts me.

You didn't have what it takes. You lacked grit.

How do you know when to persevere and when to quit?

You don't. It is always a judgment call.

Imagine a determined athlete who has spent months training for a marathon. Halfway through the race she feels a hot, sharp pain in her foot. She presses on but the pain worsens. Experienced athletes know the difference between good pain and bad pain, and this is most definitely bad pain. She can barely run now. She limps.

Should she stop?

Maybe she can endure. She can stop, stretch, and shake it out. Maybe she can still close those last miles to the finish line. Endurance racing requires tremendous toughness, and she knows how to be tough.

On the other hand, the injury might be serious, and continuing will inflict irreparable harm on her body. Maybe she will never be able to run again. If she quits, she will ice her injury and lament the setback over beers with her friends that evening. Next week she will be in physical therapy, and a few weeks after that she'll resume training. The setback will bruise her ego but she will go on to win other races.

Then again, maybe this is the most important race of her life. Her injury really is that serious, but her entire life has culminated in this one moment. Despite the swelling and the searing pain, despite the expectation of permanent disability, maybe she should give the race everything she has. She will hobble those last five miles and collapse across the finish line. The crowd will watch in astonishment and then rise to its feet in rapturous applause. She will be a legend.

Perhaps superhuman obstinacy is the price of greatness. Achilles faced this dilemma at Troy. The gods told him he could live quietly into old age or die a gruesome battlefield death and win immortal fame. After Steve Jobs died, many entrepreneurs reflected on his toxic leadership style and unhappy personal life and asked themselves if they would be willing to pay a similar price. We marvel at his accomplishments but wonder: *was it worth it?*

Perhaps the real question is not when to quit, but what price we are willing to pay.

So how do we decide?

When is quitting mere weakness? When should we push through the pain to the finish line?

Perhaps we can take comfort in recognizing that these questions do not have correct answers. We each must answer for ourselves, based on our judgment, experience, and deepest values.

Our choices are what make man great, as John Steinbeck wrote in *East of Eden*—and Mumford and Sons later put into song. Choices are man's ladder to the stars.

In these crucial moments, you make choices about what you value, what you stand for, and who you want to be. You weigh all the futures that branch out from this one point in space and time. You consider not just this one race but every race to come. No two choices will be exactly alike because no two people are exactly alike.

You do the best you can.

You choose.

This is our crowning dignity as human beings.

LONELINESS

When the pursuit of your dream is going well, excitement abounds. Everyone wants to join your effort. The sense of purpose, meaning, and belonging can be extraordinary. Supporters come alongside you, celebrate your accomplishments, and contribute. You bask in the affection and camaraderie.

When setbacks become more than setbacks, everything changes. Your relationships are tested like never before. Many unravel.

You find yourself alone, trying to hold it together while contemplating the hardest decisions of your life.

Your sense of isolation lingers even in the presence of others. Nobody can understand the weight you carry. You shrink down, retreat deep within yourself, alienated by your own sense of inadequacy.

If you are a leader, failure isolates you from your team.

Any entrepreneur relies on cofounders, partners, colleagues, employees, or volunteers. In the early days you bubble with excitement, eating late-night takeout together while charting your future. You have so many dreams and ambitions. You will change the world.

Your first setbacks draw your team even tighter. Nothing forges a band of brothers like shared hardship. You rally the troops, remind them of the stakes, and renew their determination to fight until victory.

As failures compound, however, this magical synergy evaporates. Fear infects like a cancer. Desperation strains your relationships, as each of you—under the greatest pressure imaginable—grapples with difficult, high-stakes decisions. Critical disagreements arise. Emotions run hot. Rivalries emerge.

At some point, an insidious feeling takes hold that the ship is sinking. Personal survival becomes the imperative. Key members of your team depart for other jobs. Supporters melt away. The phone stops ringing. Email slows to a trickle.

As the leader, you are left holding the bag.

Failure also isolates you from your support network.

You have family, friends, and supporters who cheered you on when you took that first, brave step into the unknown. Now that the damage is mounting and you are contemplating quitting, an awkward silence stands between you. They have no idea what to say.

Well-intended conversations can isolate you even further. Enthusiastic supporters urge you not to give up, which is great advice up until the moment that it isn't.

Other supporters will problem-solve for you. A friend will offer to connect you with his friend's brother-in-law's boss, who knows someone in the finance industry, and will be hurt when you don't jump at the chance. You will patiently listen to woefully ignorant suggestions. "I'm not so sure that will work," you will say in the kindest tone possible, your deflection based on years of deep experience. Your supporters may seem bruised by this disillusioned cynic who refuses to accept help.

You may have accepted funding or practical help from your supporters, which introduces another kind of alienation. You both know the loans will never be repaid. Every once in a while, the news profiles parents who take out a second mortgage to finance their nineteen-year-old's successful new startup. I have to wonder what happens to such families when the startups fail.

The largest donations we accepted from friends and family still haunt me. My relative who made the last-minute $5,000 donation claims no hard feelings. I hope he is telling the truth. To this day, I feel ashamed every time I see him. I withdraw deeper within myself.

Failure can wound your closest loved ones. Even if they do not directly contribute to your effort, they are typically the ones who share your burden during the hardest times.

When you are failing, you are hardly at your best. You are exhausted, stressed, and scared. Your mood swings wildly. You are never far from tears and can erupt in anger at the slightest offense.

You are fighting for survival, which makes you calloused and self-centered. You might become emotionally distant. You might snap at your partner or kids, which can fuel a cycle of guilt and resentment.

Your failure can impose practical stresses on these loved ones. Your partner might shoulder the load at home while you manage the latest crisis. You might be too exhausted for intimacy. If your health suffers, your partner might pick up the slack. You might take a catastrophic financial hit or lose your home. Your loved ones might grow depressed or angry with you because of the stresses you have imposed on their lives. You might feel angry back, or you might feel guilty for dragging them into this mess.

For years, Uplift's failure left a sore place in my marriage. Wendy gave her heart to the project, and our family made many sacrifices along the way. She also managed our donor relations during the crowdfunding campaign, so felt personally responsible when it became clear that Uplift would not recover. The trauma of that season affected us in different ways, and the memory still remains tender to the touch.

Failure damages your broader ability to connect socially. Even as the pain creates a longing for meaningful relationships, it erodes your self-confidence and creates protective barriers against being wounded again. It undermines the generous reciprocity that lies at the heart of satisfying relationships.

You are never sure how to handle yourself in social interactions. You continually debate whether to smile and say everything is fine, or show vulnerability and risk saying too much. You constantly feel on edge. You worry that your anxiety makes others uncomfortable.

Your heroic effort likely pulled you into a broader community. You got to know an industry, joined a writer's group, or made friends with other moms starting small businesses. You were all on similar journeys, all aspiring, all encouraging each other onward.

This community loves a good success story, so when you are succeeding, you find abundant opportunities to network and share your experience. Your first press coverage sets off an avalanche. Speaking invitations pour in. Budding entrepreneurs write you. Friends offer up connections. Your LinkedIn network grows.

And then, suddenly, you are a pariah.

When we dissolved Uplift Aeronautics, I envisioned receiving invitations to conferences to speak about our lessons learned. No invitation ever came. Nobody invites failures. At least, not until they've become successes again.

It's like that old trope from war movies. As fresh, smooth-skinned soldiers arrive on the battlefield, they congregate around braggarts who regale them with heroic tales. But the grizzled veterans, the ones who have looked into the dark abyss of war, who have watched friends erased from existence by a mortar round or gunfire, who carry the eternal burden of taking another man's life, sit alone by peripheral campfires.

In summary, failure can bring an encounter with loneliness like you have never known. This shadow falls during your greatest trial, when you need strength and support, when you feel trapped but have to keep showing up to fight new battles each day.

Loneliness does not endure forever. In the aftermath of failure, you will begin a long process of healing and growth. Not every relationship will heal, but many will. You will find rich new relationships as well.

However, this process cannot be rushed.

You might be here for a while.

In the meantime, you will spend a great deal of time alone. Failure takes you on a journey deep within yourself.

We turn to that journey next.

IMPOSTOR SYNDROME

When things are going well, every new success reinforces your belief in yourself. Success seems to validate your personal qualities, your decision-making, and the sweat, blood, and tears you have invested.

Failure unravels this newfound confidence. Every new setback seems to imply your own inadequacy. You failed to navigate these turbulent rapids. Now you are spinning out of control, where a better or stronger leader might have done better.

This can set off a self-destructive cycle.

Failure is usually a process, not an all-or-nothing event. You are still in the captain's seat, making crucial decisions. You might still save the effort if you play your cards right, but now your fallibility is obvious. You live in fear of making another mistake. You overanalyze. You hem and haw. You lose sleep, which leaves you exhausted and hyperemotional and impedes your judgment. You make decisions, then reverse them. You have always despised indecisiveness in leaders, so your own indecisiveness rattles you.

Doubt spreads outward from there. Team members, employees, and supporters look to you for leadership, but your self-doubt rapidly erodes their confidence. They watch with bated breath. Whispered conversations trail into silence when you walk by. At least, you think they do. Is it real, or are you paranoid now? Behind their thin smiles you imagine fear, mistrust, and a parade of silent thoughts about how you have turned into a mental case.

We have a special phrase for this kind of self-doubt. *Impostor syndrome* is the fear of being exposed as a fraud. Even in the best of times, impostor syndrome can devastate us. It fuels chronic anxiety that we are not enough, robs us of joy, and propels us onto an endless quest to prove that we have what it takes.

Impostor syndrome plagues high-success cultures. Silicon Valley is a case in point. On the surface, everybody has it together. Every day you meet CEOs, venture capitalists, and lawyers for major financial firms. After work they cycle, train for marathons, and do CrossFit. They drive Teslas and BMWs. They volunteer for the school PTA and run nonprofits on the side. My immediate neighbors at Stanford wrote machine learning algorithms for MRI scanners, ran theater productions in foreign countries, built VR educational experiences, and led expeditions to Patagonia to reconstruct ancient climate history.

Live there long enough, though, and you see beneath the surface. Real life still happens. Marriages fray. Kids act out at school. Many of those brilliant graduate students wilt at their desks, trying to shape their messy research into something that will satisfy a dissertation committee. These exceptional individuals all look at each other and think, "I do not belong here. The admissions department made a terrible mistake."

In 2017, Army Major General John Rossi took his own life two days before pinning on his third star and taking command of the U.S. Army Space and Missile Defense Command. Rossi was well-liked and had no notable failures in his commands. The U.S. Army gave him its full confidence.

Yet for years, Rossi had suffered in silence. He felt increasingly overwhelmed as he ascended the ranks. He believed he did not deserve his many honors. He became a workaholic, hoping his relentless work ethic would mask his perceived deficiencies. He carried photos of soldiers who died under his command and felt he had not done enough to save them. According to a later investigation, Rossi had an "irrational belief that he was intellectually incapable of mastering the technical aspects of the SMDC, particularly those related to space defense."[9] His deep anxiety and relentless work ethic led to severe sleep deprivation. Ultimately, afraid of being exposed as a fraud and bringing shame on his family and the Army, he died by suicide.

John Rossi judged himself by a standard that no human being could possibly meet. He carried what the actor Andrew Garfield calls the "wound of not-enough-ness."[10] Many of us carry the same wound. We project confidence and competence to avoid being exposed.

When failure strikes, impostor syndrome gets even worse.

Failure rips away the mask, allowing the world to gawk at our limitations. We can no longer hide. Failure seems to confirm all that negative self-talk. Here, finally, is the proof that we are in over our heads.

We have been found out.

Some people seem immune to impostor syndrome.

They are brash. They swagger. They believe in their own superiority. When failure strikes, they do not look inward or question their decisions. Instead, they rage. They blame. They make excuses. They evade responsibility and throw others under the bus.

These people destroy lives. They destroy organizations. Even countries.

When you realize that this sociopathic excess is the polar opposite of impostor syndrome, a little self-doubt does not look like such a bad thing.

Behind impostor syndrome lies genuine humility.

When we recognize our fallibility, we test our assumptions. We examine ourselves for deficiencies and strive for self-improvement. We seek counsel. We search for evidence to validate our decisions. We have the humility to pivot when necessary. We develop empathy for other fallible human beings.

The challenge, then, is to find that middle ground of quiet self-confidence that lies between debilitating impostor syndrome and reckless arrogance.

We know these men and women when we see them. They are grounded in values. They have a vision for themselves and the world around them. They project easy confidence within their domain of expertise while simultaneously showing curiosity, openness, and humility. They surround themselves with people who are more talented, more knowledgeable, and more capable, without a hint of insecurity. They make hard decisions in ambiguous circumstances, even knowing they will make mistakes.

This is what we should strive for.

How do we get there?

In the midst of failure, such measured self-confidence may be out of reach. You are simply trying to survive as your capsized raft careens wildly down the rapids.

Have grace on yourself. Today, survival is enough.

Take consolation in this: that when your bruised and battered body finally washes up on some rocky beach miles downriver, and you lie blinking up at the pines and the glaring sunlight, you will have learned more about yourself than many people ever do. You will have gleaned invaluable insights into your own judgment and decision-making when facing hard problems.

These lessons might take months to digest. Maybe years. But

your experience with failure will have spared you the fate of becoming just another arrogant sociopath. You will be wiser, stronger, and more capable.

You are not an impostor. You never were.

The fact you made it this far is evidence enough.

You stood in the arena and took the punishing blows. You will find your strength again and fight another round. You will be one step closer to that quiet self-confidence that we should all aspire to.

DOUBT

When you are succeeding in a difficult venture, you feel like the universe is on your side. Cosmic forces stand ready to hurl down lightning at anything that stands in your way. Your muse whispers encouragement in your ear. You are in harmony with God's will for your life.

Failure shatters this sense of divine purpose.

Religious individuals can experience this as a crisis of faith. What felt like divine benevolence now feels more like the capricious mischief of the Greek gods, smashing their favorite toy soldiers together on the killing fields of Troy. Perhaps you angered God or stepped outside his will. Perhaps He doesn't care. Maybe He doesn't exist at all.

This feeling of cosmic disharmony rattles even the non-religious. You thought you were aligned with all the benevolence of the universe, but everything changed in a moment of fickle cruelty. The universe is cold and indifferent.

When your setbacks began, you merely doubted yourself. Now you doubt your place in the universe.

As I rode out my season of failure, I often thought back to Churchill's war rooms.

I felt as if... all my life had been but a preparation for this hour and for this trial.

I had spent my life searching a cause larger than myself. In that sanctified moment in Istanbul, it all came together: my career as a U.S. Air Force cargo pilot, my Arabic language skills, my study of the Syrian civil war, my desire to be an entrepreneur, my software development skills, my childhood building robots.

This is what I had been born for. This was my quest.

Conviction burned within me like a fire. It propelled me through so many trials. I imagined how Lincoln felt, carrying the weight of the nation for five long years of civil war. Or Churchill, rallying Great Britain in its darkest hours.

And then it fell apart. That lofty sense of cosmic significance evaporated.

I had been delusional. My reflections on Churchill and Lincoln smacked of hubris. I am embarrassed to admit I had those thoughts at all.

History provides many examples of powerful and well-intended people who, in their quest to do good, unleashed terrible consequences. The titans of social media, so eager to connect us, enabled a global hate machine that has accelerated the unraveling of democracy. The George W. Bush cabinet embarked on a crusade to liberate Iraq.

What if I was no better? What if my passion, far from being a gift, was a dangerous delusion? The implications of that terrified me. If that was true, the best thing I could do for the world was stop. Stop the project. Stop dreaming. Stop trying to do great things. I should aim low, for the safe and familiar, ensuring I would not hurt anyone else.

When he was twenty-one years old, Josh Harris published a runaway bestseller titled *I Kissed Dating Goodbye*. The book urged young Evangelical Christians to renounce dating and instead embrace a highly structured process of courtship. Harris recalls praying, "God, let me write a book that will change the world." He was, in his own words, "young, zealous, certain, and restlessly ambitious."[11] His book sold more than a million copies, and he went on to become a megachurch pastor and write more bestsellers.

Unfortunately, the book set impossible standards for relationships, fueled a massive shame complex, and warped a generation's ability to have healthy relationships. Some Christians, grappling years later with divorce or struggling marriages, blamed Harris for ruining their lives.

Two decades after its release, after many meetings with people affected by his book, Harris issued a formal apology and stopped publication.[12] In video interviews he looks sad and wounded as he apologizes for the hurt he caused. One senses he has had this conversation hundreds of times, and that it hurts every time.

Harris' season of failure was not over. A year after renouncing the book, he revealed he was getting a divorce. Nine days later, he announced he no longer identified as Christian. Shocked Christians felt betrayed and called for Harris to repent.

I regard Josh Harris today with empathy and respect. In his efforts to obey a divine calling and then, later, his conscience, it appears he upset almost everyone. Yet owning his story was a necessary step in healing, both for himself and for his readers.

One Harris quote still gives me chills: "I was wrong about the biggest accomplishment of my life."[13]

Ambition frightens me now, even ambition to do good.

And yet we need it. Most people prefer safe familiarity, which can be a good thing. These people stabilize civilization, anchor us in traditions, and dampen the volatility of a turbulent world.

But ambition is the revitalizing force that drives almost every great advance in human history. It is the dreamers who launch expeditions into the unknown, some for the better and some for the worse. They invent. They found. They build. They govern. They abolish old laws and create new ones. They shatter social taboos and experiment with new ways of being.

In moments of crisis, they lead. History is made by men and women who rise to their full greatness at these exceptional junctures of history. Sometimes their efforts succeed and result in tremendous good; sometimes they fail or unleash awful consequences. Even the best leave mixed legacies.

An indifferent universe offers no guarantees.

When we fail, we learn this the hard way. It leaves us reeling.

My season of failure coincided with the last stages of my Christian deconstruction. That had profound implications for how I made sense of this cosmic uncertainty.

As a secular humanist, I no longer believed in a master plan. That conviction I had felt, that sense of divine blessing, did not come from God; it arose from within my own soul. That conviction represented the best of my humanity aligning with a unique opportunity to do something good for the world.

In some ways, this makes things easier. The nonbeliever feels no obligation to search out divine purpose. The problem of evil—the question of how to reconcile a good God with a cruel universe—ceases to be. The universe simply is. The nonbeliever's challenge is to flow with life as it comes.

When we drink from the cup of failure, we develop a fearful reverence for our ambitions. They lead us to try difficult and important things, but they offer no guarantees of success or of improving the world. We must grapple constantly with the possibility that we are wrong and could do grave damage. We learn to temper our boldness with humility.

Living with this tension is not easy, but it is both wise and right.

Religious believers must process failure differently because their worldview requires divine purpose, or at least a master caretaker.

Even if God does not foreordain events, his sovereignty somehow operates within them, unfolding his purposes in mysterious and hidden ways. If nothing else, God works through even the worst circumstances to advance some form of ultimate good.

Failure tests this worldview. It undermines our conviction that God has a specific will for our lives. This can paralyze a certain kind of believer. If I was wrong this time, he thinks, how can I ever be sure again? How can I ever know the will of God?

Perhaps this view of God's will—as railroad tracks that we can either follow or stray from—is too brittle. The truth has to be more nuanced.

Believers who emerge from such trials with strengthened faith generally learn to give up their iron-clad certainties. They relax into their brokenness, dependency, and lack of control. They learn to embrace mystery.

God offers few answers to these ultimate questions. When Job cries out in his suffering, God does not offer a reasoned argument about the problem of evil; he awes Job with a display of his power over the heavens and the earth. It is an answer, but not of the type Job was expecting. God effectively says, "Look who I am, compared to you."

The implicit message is to trust and submit. In this act of surrender to God's mystery, believers find their way forward, trusting in purposes that exceed their limited understanding.

Ultimately, then, the paths of the believer and the nonbeliever are more similar than we might think. When we confront failure, we must acknowledge the limits of our own control. We must surrender to the forces of God or the universe.

This does not mean giving up; on the contrary, it means maximizing our agency within the limited domain over which we do have control. It means investing in the absolute best parts of ourselves, so we are ready to act when the great wheel of the universe turns in our favor once again.

We can emerge from failure more supple, able to flow with events like water, shaping ourselves to every contour. We sink blissfully into the mysterious silence of God or the universe. We learn to live with grace, dignity, and strength so we can endure when failure or suffering strike again.

No catastrophe can break our spiritual foundations again. We now possess a tremendous secret. We know our place in the universe.

WEAKNESS

In summer of 1998 I began Basic Cadet Training at the U.S. Air Force Academy. I was not athletic in high school so Basic was a harrowing experience. Challenges filled each day. Mostly I endured them. I kept up on runs. I did my pushups (not always with good form). I stood placidly as upperclassmen screamed in my face about every deficiency in my physical condition, my intelligence, and my fitness to be a member of the United States Air Force.

I kept up with it all.

Except once.

One day, during a particularly grueling physical conditioning session, my body gave out. I literally could not do another drill and collapsed on the grass. Upperclassmen swarmed around me like hornets, screaming. I tried to get up again and fell. Finally they muttered in disgust and ordered me to sit by a tree, drink water, and wait. I tried to rejoin my classmates, but it was too late. Watching this sufferfest from the sidelines was my worst moment of Basic. It was the one and only time I *broke*.

The upperclassmen muttered, "Jacobsen is weak."

I still feel the shame.

Weakness destroys your sense of self-worth.

If you are strong, you can endure anything. No matter how bad things get, you can pick yourself up and get moving again.

Strength through adversity invites admiration. When an injured boxer rises, our hearts soar. We love to see underdogs overcome challenges because their stories give us hope for ourselves. We have been there before and know we will be there again. We cheer for our collective humanity.

But weakness embarrasses us.

When a boxer cannot rise from the mat, we avert our eyes. It is too painful to watch. *Get up, get up*, we groan under our breath. We want this horrible moment to be redeemed. Our hearts sink.

When we fail, the world looks away.

Weakness has a physical aspect.

Few of us can endure failure with our health intact.

Even when you are succeeding, daring greatly demands everything you have. If you want to change the world with that new company or complete that Ironman or land that dream job, you have to work hard for it

Even on your best days, you collapse into bed exhausted every night. In the morning, you plod straight to your desk or into your running shoes. On a bad day, you are lucky to sleep at all because your mind races at five hundred miles per hour at three in the morning.

Your body suffers. You do not exercise as much as you should (or exercise too much). You gain weight (or lose it). You subsist on greasy pizza (or tiny vegan portions weighed on a food scale). Whichever extreme you are at, you push your body to the limits.

Then, when you fail, your body reels.

I had always been cool and calm under pressure. My drive and energy knew no limits. I excelled at most things I tried. I prided myself on my ability to shake off setbacks, learn the appropriate lessons, and get back to work. All of that was indispensable when leading Uplift.

Yet as the torturous months accumulated, my strength flagged. Anxiety became a dull, constant companion that occasionally flared into middle-of-the-night episodes of terror. Aspects of the project became so stressful that I literally could not bear to think about them. I dreaded opening my email. I put off replies for weeks.

And then I went over the edge.

My self-confidence was destroyed. I could barely function because of the stress. My mental health collapsed. I cried. Although I never came close to acting on these feelings, I began to see the appeal of suicide.

I knew the literature about failure. I knew I should fail fast and get back to work. I knew that failure helps us grow stronger. I knew that this experience would positively shape me in many unseen ways, and that years or decades in the future, I might look back on this season with gratitude.

In the moment, none of that mattered; I was too broken down. I was that cadet at USAFA again, straining in the grass, muscles quivering, unable to grind out another pushup.

After the back injury on my 35th birthday, I began physical therapy. The therapist who greeted me that first day was an attractive, bubbly, athletic woman my age. She asked me to perform a variety of exercises so she could assess my core and back strength. She frowned, thought for a moment, and said, "Your problem is, you're just... weak."

I resolved to get strong.

By late August I felt much better. I was running again. I worked at a standing desk. I performed back and core exercises every morning. Life was still hell, but at least my body wasn't working against me.

Then I injured my IT band. My body had betrayed me a second time. Time and rest did not heal the injury.

I landed in physical therapy a second time.

Again, I resolved to get strong.

The injury healed. I began swimming. I did my first triathlon.

Then came the scabies.

I couldn't catch a break.

My flesh had come to embody all my weakness and failure. At times, I wanted to die.

Every failure experience brings these moments that take you past the limits of your strength. You forge ahead. You fight your battles. Some days you win, some days you lose, but you never stop fighting.

But every battle saps some of your strength, and there comes a moment when you simply can't lift your sword again.

It's like that scene in *The Fellowship of the Ring*, when Boromir keeps taking arrows in the chest and keeps rising to slay more Uruk-hai, until he literally cannot rise again and falls to his knees.

All the literature tells you that quitting is for the weak. Tell that to Boromir, kneeling among his enemies with three arrows in his chest.

No matter how strong you are, weakness can come for you. It comes in the moment when you issue the order to dissolve the company. When you sign the divorce papers, fall out of the triathlon, or declare bankruptcy. When you listen helplessly to a crackling radio, unable to do anything as your fellow soldiers make their last stand against an overwhelming enemy force.

When your strength fails and weakness overtakes you, it seems like the world is ending. It isn't. You can eventually find your way back to strength, or at least to an amicable truce with your body.

But you cannot rush.

That is essentially the definition of failure. You are out past the limits of your strength; you literally cannot will your way out of this.

Accept that. Rest. Heal.

Strength will come later.

BURNOUT

When you are passionate about a cause, you light up like a supernova. The energy crackles and flows. It powers you through obstacles that would make most people cower. Sheer love propels you onward.

That is where burnout begins.

The dictionary defines burnout as "exhaustion of physical or emotional strength or motivation usually as a result of prolonged stress or frustration."[14]

Yes, burnout entails exhaustion, but it signifies so much more.

Burnout is really about unrequited love.

No matter how much you love your quest, it does not always love you back. Often the world does not align behind your glorious sense of purpose. Whenever some new twist or turn puts your goal further beyond reach, you must burn ever brighter to compensate. You seethe at the injustice. You choke back tears of disappointment. Despite all that, you do what you have always done, which is to hold it together through the sheer force of love.

Eventually, this misalignment between your passion and circumstances opens a wound in your soul. Dina Glouberman writes,

> My view is that one of the major differences between depression and burnout is that depression has to do with failure and loss, while burnout has more to do with a profound disappointment

in love, meaning and our ability to be of service... Burnout comes to those who love well though not always wisely.[15]

You successfully manage the strain at first. Yes, you know you are working too hard. Yes, you are frustrated that management is not more grateful. Yes, you are angry that needed support did not materialize. But you have dealt with stress before and you can deal with it again.

Besides, it's impossible to stop now. The work must be done. Your team is depending on you. Your children need you to be strong. If you stop now, the project will fail.

When challenges arise, the first instinct of a passionate, creative, and high-energy individual is to compensate by working even harder. The same as you have always done.

Your soul tears and bleeds.

Your inner fire flickers.

Burnout presents three key signs, according to Glouberman. First, you feel chronic exhaustion—emotionally, mentally, or physically. Sleep does not help. You used to rise at five thirty every morning to write a few pages or code or get in a vigorous run before the world awoke. Now it's all you can do to drag yourself out of bed with the kids.

Maybe your first instinct is to brute force further productivity. You set an alarm. It works for a day or two but now you have dark circles under your eyes, and you yell at your kids for the slightest infraction and you spend those "productive" mornings staring bleary-eyed into the distance.

Next you try the opposite approach: prioritizing sleep. You stop setting alarms. You go to bed earlier. You take naps. Your health improves. The dark circles go away. But no matter how much sleep you get, you never feel rested. The thought of facing your project fills with you dread. You lurch through your days like a zombie.

Vacations offer no reprieve. A vacation is merely an opportunity to stew in your fragmented, anxiety-ridden thoughts in a different location while the e-mails and obligations pile up in a crushing heap. Even if you can get away, a week is hardly enough to recharge. You need months. Maybe years.

Your efforts to rest and recuperate all fail because they misdiagnose what is actually wrong. You aren't drained because you need more sleep; you suffer because you have a broken heart.

The second sign of burnout is that you increasingly feel cut off from yourself and others.

The latter is perhaps easier to diagnose. Your single-minded dedication to the cause wreaked havoc in other parts of your life. You told yourself this was a sacrifice for a higher calling. Perhaps your loved ones even agreed. Over time, however, the strain on your relationships mounts. Your marriage frays. You see friends less, and then not at all. Your single-minded passion becomes a black hole, sucking in every thought and every conversation, leaving nothing else to escape.

Isolation from self is harder to recognize in our always-connected world of fragmented attention and constant distraction. Few of us are in touch with our deepest selves to begin with.

When burnout strikes, this sense of alienation gets worse. You lose touch with your hopes and dreams for the future. Nothing excites you anymore. You have no hobbies or passions. You fear solitude. If your great cause was suddenly taken away, you would have no idea who you are.

Maybe that is why you keep fighting so hard, even with your broken heart.

You cannot imagine life without this.

You would be terrified to look in the mirror.

Glouberman's third sign of burnout is decreasing effectiveness at the things you have always done, either at work or at home.

If you are a high achiever, this might be the first thing you notice because your work is so important to you. As your energy ebbs, this vital work suffers, which instills terror and panic. You know you are breaking down, *but the work... the work!*

Your most important job right now is to stop the ship from sinking. You need to court a particular investor. You need to permanently resolve the toxic dispute in your executive team. You need to complete three late papers and a major project in the next two weeks in order to graduate. You need to muster the courage to call your estranged daughter and talk through that thing that has stood between you for the last five years.

But right now, confronting those hard problems seems impossible, because you can't even handle the basics. You drop balls. You miss key meetings and deadlines. You are prone to negative outbursts. Colleagues get angry.

You are fucking up, your inner critic scolds.

Soon this becomes something worse: *YOU are a fuck-up.*

By the time you recognize burnout in your life, it is likely too late.

Cosmetic changes to your routine will not bring you back from the brink. You suffer something much deeper and more damaging than fatigue or acute stress. Exercise, medication, or a vacation will not cure your predicament. David Whyte writes that the antidote to this kind of exhaustion is not rest; it is wholeheartedness.[16]

Your body and soul are warning you that something is profoundly wrong with the life you are imposing on yourself. Glouberman describes burnout as a circuit breaker. It trips, quite literally, to protect the body and soul from suffering further harm or even death.

Much later, as you look back on your journey, you might regard this intervention with gratitude. Your body knows how to protect itself even when your conscious mind does not. Burnout invites you on a journey of personal growth, reinvention, and even joy.

In the meantime, burnout simply hurts.

Your heart is broken.

Your fire has gone out.

Before you can even think about healing, you need to grieve.

PART THREE

AFTERMATH

OVER

At last, it is over.

You have made the decision, or it has been made for you. No more wringing of the hands. No more lying awake before dawn agonizing over the key decisions.

The dream has come to an end.

Uplift Aeronautics no longer exists. The Syria Airlift Project is over.

The hell of these last few months recedes like a thunderstorm on the bruised horizon. The wind still whips, the fierce rain still slants in your face, but you are through the worst of it. The first glimpses of blue sky crack through.

You are exhausted. You sleep untold hours, now that you can. You cry at the slightest thought. You pass through your days like a ghost.

It is tempting to think that failure is done with you, and that you will at last know some peace. But fortune is a trickster, and she is not yet ready to let you go.

You are not better.

You are simply unmoored.

HAS-BEEN

Success assures you that your life matters for something. Most of us go through life terrified that it doesn't. We wake up one day in our thirties or forties, look back over the past few decades, and wonder what the hell we are doing with our lives. We ask what we have accomplished, what great loves we have known. We fear mediocrity. We suspect that our closest loved ones shake their heads behind our backs at the disappointments we have brought.

When you are succeeding in a new venture, you briefly transcend that chronic, nagging sense of irrelevance.

At a superficial level, success strokes your ego, but validation goes much deeper than ego satisfaction. You know the pride of accomplishment, for one thing. You engaged in the sacred act of creating something that never previously existed. You invested so much, and did it in a community of belonging.

Every type of effort has its success metrics. Businesses want positive cash flow. Nonprofits want impact. Artists want sales, readers, or glowing reviews. We do not chase these metrics merely for riches or glory; we see them as measures of value.

They feel like measures of *our* value.

You exist.

And then it's over.

One of the most chilling aspects of life after failure is the silence.

After the Stanford fire, I braced for negative news coverage and phone calls inviting me to appear before angry Stanford administrators. Neither ever came. When we sent a grim donor update offering to refund donations, we heard none of the frustration, anger, and disappointment I anticipated. When we announced the dissolution of Uplift Aeronautics five months later, we heard crickets.

I felt relieved that my worst fears were not realized, but it was disconcerting how fast the world moved on.

This is life as a has-been.

You are she who must not be named.

It's like being invisible, or a ghost. You run frantically around work or school and wave your arms in people's faces and say "Here I am! I exist!" but nobody can see you or hear you. Your earlier sense of validation feels like a ruse. All your worst fears about your value as a human being come roaring back.

You are a disappointment, a mediocre human being who is padding slowly towards the grave. You have wrought real damage. You have wasted people's money. You have disrupted the lives of your employees, your volunteers, and your family. You nearly burned down Stanford.

Nobody remembers the things you accomplished, the good that was taking form, the universe of potential you worked so hard to unleash.

"People treat it as if it never happened, as if it never had value," Avni Patel Thompson says, referencing the shutdown of a company she gave four years to. "It's like it never existed." That erasure from existence, she says, is the most painful part of a shutdown.[17]

When we dissolved Uplift, our closest supporters immediately stopped referencing our story. A partner organization published a book-length report on the state of humanitarian drones. We did not merit a footnote. Another supporter published a newspaper op-ed calling for humanitarian drone airdrops in Syria. He listed numerous initiatives that showed the promise of drone technology but did not mention the Syria Airlift Project. Given his level of involvement before, it was not a moment of forgetfulness. Stanford Magazine ran a glowing 3000-word article on all the amazing drone research on campus. Other than a sentence about the fire, we did not receive a single mention.

We were an embarrassment now. We were being excised from history.

"What do you expect?" one former volunteer said. "We didn't achieve what we tried to do."

She wasn't being cruel or calloused. She was giving me the truth, like a bucket of cold water in my face.

This silence plays out in any domain.

Maybe you get fired from the company where you have worked for the past three years. Other than two friends who take you out for beers, you don't hear another word from the dozens of colleagues you worked with.

Your debilitating sports injury invites a short-lived wave of sympathy from friends and then everybody moves on.

Nobody is being cruel. This is just the way of the world. Everyone is swamped, and beholding failure is awkward and energy-draining. The world snaps back from it like a hand from a hot stove.

One of my favorite places to work is the courtyard outside Stanford's Graduate School of Business (GSB). You can sit in warm sunlight. A parade of fascinating people stroll through. You can eavesdrop on cutting-edge scientific research and hear ten different languages spoken. At any given moment, numerous businesses take shape around you.

As the Executive Director of Uplift Aeronautics, I had countless coffees at GSB with supporters, journalists, engineers, business leaders, and students. Aspiring entrepreneurs hung on my every word.

After the fire, I continued to work out of GSB, mostly on my dissertation, usually alone. Nobody sought meetings anymore.

I still eavesdropped on those conversations in which Stanford students birthed companies on the backs of napkins. Many involved drones. These students had big ideas, big promises, and in some cases big egos. I knew now what was entailed in building a viable business, and I knew most of them did not have a chance. Yet they kept plugging away, and investors kept giving them millions, and they kept imploding.

I sat back with folded arms, watching from a distance. Nobody asked my opinion. I was just another washed-up grad student in the coffee shop, plugging away on his MacBook. I couldn't possibly have anything to say.

When you are a has-been, you have to confront an ugly reality: you *do* have an ego. Maybe you don't crave the limelight, but you do want to be validated. Maybe you don't seek fame, but you do want respect and love. Maybe you don't want to be a celebrity, but you do want acknowledgement for those years of work.

It doesn't matter how saintly and selfless you are: we all have the snarling demon of ego inside. When you become a has-been, that demon will not be fed. It will be ravenous, starving, clawing its way out of you. You have two options: you can let it eat you alive, or you can fight to transcend it.

We have all met has-beens who never tamed their egos. At

cocktail parties they regale you with tale after tale of faded accomplishments. They name-drop celebrities they brushed with, books they read, investors they courted, professors they studied with. They are like fishermen casting different kinds of bait, desperately hoping for a catch.

Ravenous ego can also express itself through bitterness, which is equally unattractive. These people rage against those who let them down. They fantasize about how things might have turned out differently. They refuse to take responsibility for their mistakes. They vent their anger to every captive audience life hands them.

You want to be better than that.

So you sit there at your own equivalent of GSB, latte in hand, watching the busy world spin, contemplating these aspiring and successful individuals who are too busy with their own ambitions to care about your dream or its failure. You flip through the latest trade magazine and muse about your own absence from its pages. One way or another, you learn to be okay with that.

It isn't easy.

But if you can find your way through this, you will be better for it. Failure teaches you to do battle with your own ego. It is an unlikely gift but perhaps the most important that failure offers.

ANGER

Failure gives you a lot to be angry about.

Sometimes your anger is justified; sometimes it is not. Much of the time you aren't sure, so your anger becomes another source of self-doubt.

Anger is a curious emotion. It is decidedly unpleasant, and studies correlate anger with a host of negative health outcomes like headaches, indigestion, insomnia, depression, high blood pressure, and even heart attacks and strokes. Anger swamps the soul and makes it impossible to feel positive emotions like peace, joy, or love.

Even so, we crave anger like a drug. On a clear sunny day, we can summon it out of nowhere like dark magic and whip it into a frenzied storm. Once summoned, it feeds on itself, calling us to ever-greater depths of rage. We *want* to feel angry. Like lust, anger makes vain promises of ever-greater satisfaction.

We know it's a lie, and yet we want to believe it.

In our clear-minded moments, we know anger will destroy us if we let it. We have all met old, hardened, wounded people who have spent a lifetime internalizing their contempt. It literally becomes etched into the lines of their faces.

We want to rise above that, but it is so hard to let go.

One source of anger is other people.

Failure usually results from innumerable human decisions. As you mentally replay your journey, you note a hundred points where things might have gone differently. You find so many people to blame. Cofounders who made disastrous decisions. Your stubborn and uncompromising spouse. Your troubled teenager. The investor who turns you down at a critical moment. Customers who hate your product. Regulators who shut you down.

Having someone to blame conveniently alleviates us of responsibility. In the most extreme cases, a hapless bystander to our derailment can become the target of our rage. We have a special word for people who project anger this way: *assholes*. Think of the first-class businessman berating an airline agent because he missed his flight. Amplify the stakes and time horizons and you will find elite ranks of assholes who destroy companies or lead generations of young men to violent deaths in foreign lands.

In *The Great Divorce*, C.S. Lewis' fictional interpretation of heaven and hell, two travelers witness a damned Napoleon pacing up and down the halls of his house for eternity, muttering, "It was Soult's fault. It was Ney's fault. It was Josephine's fault. It was the fault of the Russians. It was the fault of the English."[18] Napoleon is imprisoned within a hell of his own making.

Rage's impotence is most obvious when there is no one to blame.

Often times, failure results from bad luck.

In 2013 a leased Naval hangar collapsed in Tustin, California, destroying the $65 million airship prototype belonging to Aeroscraft Aeronautical Systems and derailing a $3 billion funding round.[19] That is bad luck.

History can hinge on rolls of the dice. Wars are won and lost because of mud; a few inches can impede artillery or armor and leave infantry exposed to slaughter. Soldiers quickly learn that war is careless, random, and indifferent.

Bad luck provokes rage, but it is helpless rage. After the Persian emperor Xerxes completed an immense project to bridge the Hellespont, a storm destroyed everything. Xerxes flew into a rage and ordered his troops to whip the ocean with chains while uttering hateful curses.[20]

It is amusing, reading about the greatest of kings reduced to such pathetic fury. Yet we have all been there.

When bad luck destroys our fortune, we whip the metaphorical sea with our own chains. In high school, a basketball-playing friend of mine punched a wall after missing a critical basket. He broke his hand and was down for months.

I am no better. When my back injury flares up, I sulk and pout and can snap at my wife and children. I am embarrassed to say I did it this morning. I flush at my own hypocrisy as I write, squirming in my desk chair, cursing the pain rippling wavelike through my lower back.

Given that Lake Lagunita is a tinderbox and drone batteries are so flammable, I still wonder why it was my team that started the fire—we with our meticulous preparations, detailed checklists, rigorous design practices, and a total commitment to flight safety.

A couple months after the fire, after the Stanford drone club quietly eased us out, I watched some students aggressively maneuver a cobbled-together quadcopter through the air. The highly flammable battery, which they had sloppily attached with Velcro, was hurled free, sailed overboard, and plummeted to a crash landing in the dry tinder a hundred feet below. The students hooted at their silly recklessness. Of course *that* battery didn't catch fire.

If we can make it past those ego-protecting defenses of blame and deflection, we come to an even deeper source of anger: ourselves. At the end of the day, we were in the captain's chair, and we made plenty of mistakes of our own.

Once we can admit that, our shortcomings become glaring. We did not spot the fatal flaw. We did not intervene at the crucial moment. We did not fire that obviously toxic employee who would soon destroy everything. We were cruel and ungrateful to our girlfriend, or provoked our teenager and drove her away. We got behind the wheel when we were just *a little* buzzed.

So we rage. We whip ourselves with Xerxes' chains.

Like the other emotions associated with failure, we cannot rush anger. It must, in some sense, run its course. And yet we cannot afford to let it rule us—not if we want to get on with our lives and become good, generous, joyful people again. We must feel the anger, observe it, and listen to what it can teach us, but commit to move past it.

Self-reflection is essential. We must assess the degree to which our anger is actually justified. We must have the presence of mind to recognize blame and deflection, and admit when our anger is misguided. We must take an honest inventory of our own contributions to failure.

In some cases, we suffered real wrongs and need to seek justice or restitution. The call to tame anger is not a call to be a pushover. Some measure of anger can fuel our pursuit of justice, but we must recognize that we are playing with fire. Humanity's greatest and most inspiring leaders—Jesus, Gandhi, Martin Luther King Jr., Nelson Mandela—found ways to advance justice while refusing to succumb to bitterness.

I wish I could tell you how to get there, but I am still learning myself. I can only tell you that we need to try. Our lives depend on it.

HURT

When you are struggling through failure and its aftermath, you can always find someone who has it worse. This raises an entirely new form of self-doubt: the doubt that you have the right to hurt.

Even as I was at my worst—my nonprofit failing, my body injured, my academic progress in question—I recognized that I was an Air Force pilot living in Silicon Valley, earning a taxpayer-funded PhD at Stanford, alongside my wonderful wife and three beautiful, healthy children.

What possible right did I have to hurt?

Many people reinforced that message. Just weeks after the fire, as I rode out my personal breakdown, an Air Force supervisor needled me for whining about my poor, sad life at Stanford. He was good-natured and jocular. He meant well, but he had absolutely no idea.

This guilt, self-denial, and external judgment is common among high achievers who struggle with depression, anxiety, and other manifestations of failure. Elizabeth Day, podcast host and author of *How to Fail*, says that the most mean-spirited review she ever received accused her of not failing or suffering enough.[21] Her guest, Glennon Doyle, recounts similar criticism. Yes, they are privileged, they acknowledge, but what does it even mean to suffer enough to earn a voice, and who gets to decide?

When we lose our right to hurt, we are denied the deepest truths of our lives. We become alienated from our own inner journeys. If we cannot hurt, we cannot heal.

A month after the fire, I talked with a friend who had an equally difficult time integrating into graduate student life. We both suffered from impostor syndrome. Neither of us felt like we belonged in our department. She was female and an ethnic minority, which created challenges that I as a white male could only abstractly comprehend. She had also unexpectedly lost her mother over the summer. When I asked her how she was holding up, she expressed her grief. She described the battle to hold her family together, even as she struggled with the weight of her PhD.

Then she asked me how I was doing.

I stammered. I had never been so aware of my own privilege.

She pushed.

I told her that my problems were so minor compared to the loss of her mother. I had no right to be having a hard time.

"You can't do that," she gently scolded. "Everyone's pain hurts."

By giving me permission to hurt, she engaged in a generous and true act of friendship. We went on to discuss my struggles with Uplift's failure, my PhD studies, and my unraveling mental health. But it still felt wrong. Reflecting on that somber car ride, I still feel the guilt like a hard knot in my stomach.

When you are in the military, you meet plenty of people who have it worse. As a C-17 pilot, I lived a grinding lifestyle that included 200+ days of travel a year, agonizingly long flying days, and permanent jet lag. My marriage felt the strain of my constant absence. I frequently flew to Afghanistan and Iraq, where I grappled with the moral weight of two failed wars. I yearned for both inner and outer peace.

Every time I started feeling sorry for myself, life slapped me in the face. In Iraq I loaded up a contingent of Army soldiers who had just spent fifteen months patrolling the streets of Baghdad. I met men and women who had limbs blown away by roadside bombs. I transported a young woman out of Afghanistan mere hours after she learned that her husband, an Army soldier, had been killed in Iraq.

On one occasion we loaded up the casket of a fallen Special Forces soldier on a frozen parking ramp in Kandahar. He had been killed in a mountain tunnel by a Taliban fighter who was using his own wife as a human shield. This soldier's band of brothers stood in a ragged formation, wearing cargo pants and thick beards and thousand-yard stares, crying like babies. One third of their unit had been killed, one man at a time, over the previous year.

You wonder who the hell *you* are to feel pain.

In extreme cases, your own failure might have harmed or killed others. In those cases, it might be even harder to give yourself permission to feel pain. What possible right do you have?

An Army friend once confided his greatest regret from years of service in Iraq: authorizing an airstrike on the wrong house. He became visibly emotional as he told the story. I suspect that wound will never fully heal.

I imagine that he has dark moments when he questions his own pain. An innocent family is dead, while he goes home each day to his wife and children.

Healing takes time. This means that pain endures long after external circumstances seem to warrant it. That only compounds your doubt about your right to experience it.

Five years have passed since Uplift dissolved. My friends and colleagues moved on. I overcame my academic challenges, earned my PhD, and went on to found and lead Rogue Squadron. My marriage is strong, and my family is healthy and happy. Even so, my sense of personal failure never lurks far beneath the surface. Friends and family are sympathetic but bewildered. I have no rational reason to feel this way.

How long is healing supposed to take?

Even as I privately fight my personal demons, I continue to meet people who endure far greater challenges than me. I have friends going through divorces. Others are losing their jobs, or want to change careers but feel trapped by their age, responsibilities, and the dire state of the economy. Two friends have taken their lives.

I need to knock it off, I think.

I need to stop pretending I'm hurting.

All I can do is circle back to that conversation with my friend, who so graciously and compassionately gave me permission to struggle, even as she was grappling with a deeper and harder grief.

Perhaps that is the best any of us can do: recognize that everyone's pain hurts, give each other the freedom to feel what they feel, and extend compassion and charity to others around us.

This grace is dangerously countercultural in today's world. We live in an age of permanent outrage. Political polarization is tearing democratic society apart, as social media amplifies our righteous indignation at each other. We routinely demonize our enemies and gatekeep each other's deepest experiences. The far right refuses to allow Blacks to feel the pain of slavery's dreadful legacy; after all, slavery is water under the bridge, and we all need to move on. The far right likewise denies the deepest lived experiences of gay, transgendered, or other minority peoples. At the same time, the far left refuses to allow white males to feel any pain of their own; white privilege is somehow supposed to inoculate them against suffering. Denied the most basic right to feel what we feel, we lash out at each other, somehow forgetting that we are all in this together.

The foundational virtues of the great religions—grace, compassion, forgiveness, charity, kindness—look as relevant as ever. Grappling with our own pain can teach us to appreciate the pain of others. I hope that I can extend to others the same kindness that my friend extended to me.

SHARING

For some of us, one of the torments of recovery is the need to talk.

Talking can help you work through your emotions and distill lessons from the ruin. You have so much to process. Talking and writing serve as psychological relief valves; they release the storm bottled within you.

Sometimes you want to reminisce, remind yourself what you achieved, and give yourself something to be proud of. The aftermath of failure often involves a kind of accounting as you tally wins and losses. When you talk with others, you find that all was not in vain. The ledger testifies to your unassailable dreams, growth, learning, and achievements. You orient on these shards of success like a mariner glimpsing stars through broken overcast.

Sometimes you simply need to vent. You want to rage against those competitors with inferior products and deceptive marketing campaigns who rake in millions. You want to pour out your frustration at being reduced to a has-been. You want someone to vindicate all this raw emotion, or at least help you excise it from your soul. Rational or not, this cathartic process is part of healing.

You have all these reasons to want to share.

And here's the rub: nobody wants to hear it.

That sounds callous. Let me clarify.

Talking about failure is not comfortable for other people.

Perhaps your own pain distresses others. Such was the case with my religious deconstruction, which directly threatened many of the people I love most. I remember what it was like, as a struggling Christian, trying to hang on to the last tattered shreds of my faith, whenever some hero or role model walked away from belief. It felt like a sword thrust to my soul. I never wanted to hurt my loved ones that way. And yet I needed friends, needed to share, needed people to walk alongside me.

The feelings associated with failure can be so bleak that they scare you. They can also scare the people who care about you. I regret a couple occasions in which I overshared and triggered anxiety in friends who were already struggling with their own battles.

These conversations can also expose the rawest, ugliest parts of yourself. How do you talk about feelings of being forgotten or overlooked without sounding whiny and egotistical? How do you talk about anger and vindictiveness without sounding like a terrible human being?

It takes a rare friend to process this with you, giving you permission to be your absolute worst. But the alternative is bottling it all up, letting it eat away at you like cancer of the soul.

Some of us don't feel the need to share; instead, we turn inward. If we correctly reason through this, we think, we can heal on our own. We view our brains as machines for intellectual calculation, with emotions tacked on as a kind of troublesome afterthought that we can wrangle under control.

Neuroscience shows us that we have this backwards. The deepest core of the brain focuses on survival and meeting basic needs. Wrapped around that is the limbic system, our emotional self. Our evolutionary ancestors did not reason through life; they quite literally *felt* their way through life, guided by emotions like pleasure and fear. Only later did the cerebral cortex evolve, allowing us to temper emotion with rational thought.

Failure plunges through all these layers like a railroad spike, right into that primitive lizard brain. It activates our fear center, threatens our survival, and triggers fight-or-flight reflexes. Once those primeval neurons are firing, reason goes out the window. We cannot simply will ourselves to override emotions with rational calculation, any more than we can will ourselves into happiness in the midst of a heated argument.

Even the most cerebral among us must *feel* our way through failure.

That is one reason why other people play an essential role in healing. Humans connect at the limbic level. They listen. They receive. They sympathize. They reassure. They embrace.

At a chemical level, the love of friends and family floods our brains with oxytocin, which helps us develop healthy attachment to other people, cultivate trust, reduce stress, sleep better, and feel safe and content.

Humans have a remarkable capacity for *limbic resonance*, which means that their emotional states are contagious. When we are fraying, the steady compassion of a friend works a kind of magic in our own brains, instilling a similar compassion within us. The phenomenon appears to be rooted in "mirror neurons" that fire in response to what other people do and express.

Buddhist teacher Jack Kornfield writes:

> Each time we meet another human being and honor their dignity, we help those around us. Their hearts resonate with ours in exactly the same way the strings of an unplucked violin vibrate with the sounds of a violin played nearby.[22]

It is a beautiful metaphor for true friendship.

We need human companions to transform our interior emotional landscape. When we share with an empathetic friend, our brains and our lives change.

If you are fortunate, you have a few beloved friends or family members who will sit with you in your hour of trial. They will listen, receive, and reassure with compassion. They will do so willingly and graciously, because your very act of coming to them testifies to the value you place on their friendship. It is their privilege and honor to be a source of strength for you.

A few close friends came to my side when I needed to share. My friend Sam responded to my religious deconstruction with profound love, friendship, and grace. My friends Emily and Elliott repeatedly checked in on me. My friend Pete, a busy Air Force officer and father, shared his own story of a startup failure in a kind and thoughtful email. They listened without judgment.

Such friends are wonderful.

But even as we lean on such friends, we must be mindful that few people *want* to carry one another's heaviest burdens. It is a task that life asks of us but not one we necessarily seek. When we invite others into the heart of our failure, we draw upon a finite reservoir of energy from someone who is fighting battles of his or her own.

Leaning on the strength of loved ones is a privilege, but one that we must exercise with care. We all know people who destroy friendships with their insatiable neediness. That is not who we want to be.

That is the dilemma. You need to share like you need to breathe, but sharing can make you feel burdensome and dangerous. So you lurch from one extreme to the other, bottling up hurts, venting them in fiery outbursts, recoiling again from the harm you have done. Self-doubt consumes you during every conversation.

Just like every other aspect of healing and recovery, you get through.

Your dearest loved ones get through with you.

There are rarely right or wrong answers in this space. That is the beauty and challenge of human relationships. Even if you overstep, even if your sharing poses a challenge to others, this becomes a part of their own journey through life. James Hollis writes:

> Despite how risky love is, how easily we are hurt, none of us can run from risking the dangerous shoals of love, compassion, and openness to others, lest we live a sterile, unrelated life, locked within the constricted frames of our history and our comfort zones. The paradox of relationship will always be that rather than solve our problems for us, relationship brings us new problems, new complexities, but that we also grow immensely from these problems, these complexities. In short, the greatest gift of relationship proves to be that as the result of encountering each other, we are obliged to grow larger than we had planned.[23]

Hopefully, one or five or twenty years from now, you can repay the kindness and generosity of your loved ones by being a rock for others in their time of need. That is how our species has always survived. We form interdependent communities. We lean on each other, and are leaned upon, in hours of need.

AFTERSHOCKS

They say that time heals all wrongs. But how much time?

Just when you think you are getting better, some new trigger can send you tumbling back into the abyss. It can take days or weeks to climb out again.

I call these aftershocks, and they have a variety of triggers. Reminders of your failed dream can make you stagger. You feel physically ill when you find an old business card or startup t-shirt. Photos of your happy days as a couple plunge you into loneliness and misery. Your chest tightens when you look at your tennis racket, guitar, or baseball mitt. Any time your industry or university appears in the news, you panic.

Minor setbacks in other areas of your life, which have nothing to do with your failure, can also devastate you. You are still weakened, hurting, and raw. You see yourself through a lens of deficiency and shame.

Your advisor has harsh feedback on your latest chapter? You are an impostor and an embarrassment who never should have been accepted into this graduate program. Your husband snaps at you for being late to pick up the kids? You are a disgrace of a mother who will never get her shit together. You unwittingly offend a subordinate at work? You were never suited for a managerial role and the company made a dreadful mistake by promoting you.

The success of others can be a powerful trigger, especially in a social media age that forces us to compare our messy, problematic, real lives against the curated projections of everybody else. You just endured the trial of your life, but there is Amanda with her perfectly tanned legs extended on a beach in Cozumel, mojito in hand. Jake and Rachel are in a photo booth, wearing stupid hats and oversized sunglasses, looking as happy as teenage lovebirds. Enrique just finished his third marathon. Nandita just published a book. Nathan is "humbled" to announce his promotion to regional manager. Chris is speaking at a high-profile software development conference. And so it goes.

You scroll on and on, unable to stop, your brain hooked on a cocktail of both dopamine hits and flight-or-fight triggers. You want to be happy for your friends, but you feel alone, inadequate, and miserable. *What am I doing with MY life?* you wonder, as this carefully staged presentation of life's finest moments rolls endlessly by. Bad chemicals flood your brain. A chain reaction spreads. Nuclear meltdown ensues.

The force of these aftershocks can be considerable.

During my final Christmas break from Stanford, I received my autumn grades and discovered that my advisor had assigned an "N" for my dissertation credits. I was horrified; he was so dissatisfied with my progress that he awarded me "no credit." This was only a couple weeks after the meeting in which he had reviewed all my work and found it sorely deficient. Without those credits, I would not graduate on time.

I was home with my parents at their beautiful lakeside house, where I should have been drinking steaming cups of apple cider, watching sunsets with my wife over the lake, and decorating Christmas cookies with my children.

Instead, my world crumbled. I staggered around the house in a daze. Exercise did not help. I sank lower and lower, heart rate spiking, emotions darkening. I ended the evening wrapped in multiple blankets, shivering, teeth chattering, so lost in my inner darkness that I couldn't do anything except sit and manage my physical symptoms.

In the morning my senses returned. It occurred to me to log on onto Stanford's registrar webpage and actually review the grading system. Much to my chagrin, I discovered that a grade of "N" did not indicate "no credit"; it indicated "satisfactory progress in a course that has not yet reached completion."

The shattered ruins of my universe reassembled themselves, like a film played in rewind.

This whole episode is highly embarrassing, but it was real. That is what aftershocks can do.

Understanding this dynamic is half the battle.

If you know aftershocks are a normal part of the healing process, you can anticipate them and recognize them when they strike. You are not broken, but you *are* wounded and healing. Understanding that gives you permission to extend a little grace to yourself.

You learn to recognize and avoid your personal land mines.

Sometimes this means avoiding particular places or people. Twice since graduating from Stanford, I have visited the meeting room where Political Science students present their work to assembled faculty and students. I always found these presentations ruthless and unsparing, even if that was not the intent. When I returned to that empty room after graduating, I felt powerful physical symptoms: racing heart, tightness in the chest, nausea, and cold sweats. Now that I recognize what that place does to me, I have no plans to ever return.

You might need to regulate your online browsing habits. Maybe you even need to go cold turkey with social media, because feeds of bedazzling success are a surefire ticket into your inner darkness.

With experience, you learn to endure aftershocks when they do come. You know that reasoning through them is impossible, because your emotions swamp your intellect. You abstractly know that you are comparing the worst in yourself to the best in others, and that they probably feel just as shitty and envious as you do. In the moment, none of that matters. All you can do is cling to the knowledge that this, too, shall pass.

Time might not heal all wrongs, but it does help. Maybe the trauma associated with failure loses its grip on you as the months turn to years, or maybe you simply get better at managing yourself.

On your better days, you accept these aftershocks as gifts. An aftershock is a warning from deep within your subconscious. An inner circuit breaker is tripping again, protecting you from further injury. *You have been here before*, your body says. *You never want to be here again.* This is a generous and good act on the body's part to help us avoid pain and live healthy lives.

One type of therapy teaches individuals to be gentle and patient with these reactions. We can recognize that the danger has passed, unclench our teeth, and take a deep breath. We can gently thank the body for its intervention to protect us. But we can also acknowledge that our lives are different now, and it is okay to feel safe.

FALSE STARTS

When you fail, your first instinct is often to get back in the ring. Sometimes this is exactly the right move. You are showing grit. You are keeping on.

But sometimes this is a devastating mistake, which just sets you up for an entirely new round of failure.

Healing takes time and maddening discipline. It forces you to move slower, be less ambitious, settle for less than you know you are capable of.

Athletes know this. When you suffer an injury, the last thing you want is to rush your recovery. It doesn't matter how grand your goals or ambitions are. If you ignore your body's warning signs, you can do irreparable damage. You might never be able to participate in your sport again.

Do not be deceived. You are not resuming training; you are making false starts.

After we nearly burned down Stanford, we did the right thing and slowed down. There would be no more sprints. No more "Hail, Mary!" passes for extraordinary victories on accelerated timelines. We would rest, recover, and settle in for the long haul at a more sustainable pace.

I spent a month just healing. I enjoyed time with family and friends. I read books for pleasure. I spent time outdoors. I focused on academic writing with renewed vigor and found myself enjoying it immensely.

I started to feel better. I got stronger. My emotions stabilized. By autumn I wanted to get back to work. Most of the team was still scattered so I focused on a solo project that I knew I would enjoy: writing a new drone ground control station in Python. I vividly remember a weekend getaway to Yosemite, huddling bleary-eyed over my laptop at 5 am, implementing new features before my family awoke. Stanford was in full swing. I was overloading on credits. I had a major paper due in the spring.

After a frenzied month, my efforts came to an abrupt stop. I had done it again; I worked myself right into another breakdown.

I resigned from Uplift. Life moved on. I found a measure of calm and serenity I hadn't known in years.

I felt better. I started to work harder. Visions swirled in my head.

I had the ingenious idea of buying my own personal drone, working on my own schedule, and taking the next steps to advance our drone delivery paradigm—without the pressure of running an organization beholden to stakeholders. Of course, I would also have no team or institutional support, but who needs that? I found my vinyl Uplift banner and considered hanging it up again.

While I waited for the drone to arrive, I explained my plan to a friend. His expression went blank as he pondered how to diplomatically tell his friend that he was a complete dumbass.

Finally he said, "Are you sure this isn't like a romantic breakup?"

I understood his meaning in an instant.

We have all had friends in tortured on-and-off relationships. I have been there myself. The relationship is falling apart and hearts are breaking, but the possibility of loss is terrifying. It is an anguishing place to be, with so much raw emotion and uncertainty clouding everything. You make a decision, second-guess yourself, and then reverse. You have breakup talks and make-up talks and then more breakup talks. You cry. You pray. You lounge around depressed.

And then, when you finally let the relationship go, you feel an unbelievable sense of lightness. You wonder what took you so long. As time goes by, and you look back on that anguished season with a little more objectivity, you can't believe you put yourselves through so much hell for a relationship that was never right to begin with.

I saw all that in a flash.

The drone and components arrived. I carefully unboxed it all. I stared at the pieces arranged on my workbench and felt my lungs constrict. The drone went back in the box, where it remains to this day.

We all know the term "rebound relationship", which is when you initiate a new romantic relationship in the aftermath of a breakup, before you have worked through all the accompanying feelings. Rebound relationships help us avoid facing loss, grief, or rejection but often entail shame and desperation.

We could apply this concept to almost any domain that touches on our passions. When we fail, we want to quickly move past the pain. We want to feel wholehearted again. We see dazzling opportunities around us and our hearts soar.

But beware false starts.

If we plunge headlong into new opportunities before we are healthy again, we risk compounding failure. Our lives may become colored with sad desperation. I knew one entrepreneur for whom founding startups was like heroin. He compulsively flitted from idea to idea, bleeding his savings on patents and custom company t-shirts, desperately hunting for his unicorn while his family unraveled. He divorced, abandoned his child, and left the country seeking his fortune elsewhere. He is too busy to be sad.

This is not to say that you will never return to writing, running, your dissertation, a romantic relationship, or a new startup. Life does go on. You will always return to where your heart calls you.

But beware false starts.

Slow down. Process. Let your experience run its course. Life's demand of you right now is to renew your strength. Settle in. Enjoy the process as best you can.

You will re-enter the ring. I promise. Just not yet.

WILDERNESS

When you are recovering from failure, you rarely know what to do next. Aftershocks continue to rattle you. Every time you think you are ready to move ahead, a False Start ensnares you.

This thing you failed at gave your life structure, purpose, and meaning. You knew exactly where you were going. You blazed with purpose. You set and achieved goals. Your relationships felt solid and secure. You knew who you were and what you were about, and the world applauded.

When you failed, all that changed. You became unmoored from your own hopes and dreams. Ambiguity and uncertainty replaced purpose.

Now you have no idea what to do.

Welcome to the wilderness.

The wilderness is a dry and arid place with little greenery or water. You are largely alone on your inner journey, even if other people surround you. The quiet is disconcerting. Freed from ambition and goals, you have little to actually *do*. The wilderness is a place to *be*.

Finding yourself in the wilderness can be terrifying.

There is good news.

The wilderness is an extraordinary place with wonders of its own. You are hardly the first person to find yourself here. The wilderness is where souls are forged. In the wilderness you make momentary contact with ultimate reality, whether you call that God or transcendence or the connectedness of all things. In the wilderness you learn to let go of every fleeting achievement, possession, and relationship, and learn that simply *being* is enough. You find inner strength that you never knew you possessed.

Nearly every major Bible character spent a season in the wilderness, maturing into a prophet. Moses lived in desert exile before leading an enslaved nation to liberation. Elijah took refuge in a desert, drinking from a brook and being fed by ravens. John the Baptist spent thirty years in the desert beyond Galilee. Mary and Joseph fled with Jesus into exile in Egypt. Jesus himself spent forty days in the desert sparring with Satan.

We find similar accounts in our great myths and in other religions. After ten years at war, Odysseus suffered another ten years in a wilderness journey before he found his way home. Mohammad received his revelations in the desert. Joseph Smith led his followers west into the desert in search of a new life.

The power and consistency of this experience is extraordinary. Wilderness forged these men like blades. They needed that strength because their callings demanded so much of them. They led unruly peoples, confronted kings, demolished power structures, and founded kingdoms.

Many modern leaders have spent their own season in the wilderness. Nelson Mandela spent 27 years in jail, fortifying his character and learning to transcend bitterness and vengeance before leading South Africa out of apartheid. Alexander Solzhenitsyn spent eight hellish years in the Gulag before writing timeless humanist literature. Martin Luther King Jr. lived in a veritable desert—consumed by depression, guilt, and fear—during his years of activism. Following the Birmingham bombing that killed four young girls, he publicly said that Blacks faced a "midnight of oppression" and confessed that his own leadership was "doing nothing, going nowhere."[24]

Lesser men would have shirked from these noble callings, but the wilderness experience transformed and empowered these men. They burned with holy fire.

The wilderness is a frightening place to be, at least at first.

You will feel lost and afraid. Thorns and brambles will tear at you. You will bleed. You will be desperate for water. You will wonder how you ever landed here, what you ever did wrong.

In the heart of that wilderness, you will face a choice. You can stew in bitterness and anger, hardening into a warped shadow of your former self. Or you can embrace the journey into this dark unknown and let it work its quiet transformation within you. You can emerge nourished by something powerful and hidden in that dark place, transformed, at peace with yourself, more ready than ever to return to the world.

As Hazrat Inayat Khan writes, "There can be no rebirth without a dark night of the soul, a total annihilation of all that you believed in and thought that you were."[25]

And rebirth is what we are after.

This dark night of the soul lies at the heart of the wilderness. It is the inner journey that mirrors our outer journey through the desert places.

The term originates with the Spanish Catholic mystic St. John of the Cross, and refers to an experience of emptiness, isolation, and utter disconnection from the Divine. What makes these seasons so difficult, St. John writes, is not so much their aridity but our fear that we have lost the path entirely and will never know spiritual blessings again.[26] Nothing gives us pleasure or joy, and we lose hope that we will ever regain our lost capacities.

The image holds power even if you do not consider yourself religious. You encounter the dark night of the soul when you lose your sense of place in the universe, when life strips away your identity, when frameworks and beliefs collapse that previously structured your life. You are disconnected from familiar roles, rituals, and sources of meaning. You feel like Dante in his opening lines of *The Inferno*, trembling as he recalls the terror of being lost in a dark wood.

All your old certainties are gone.

You no longer know who you are.

My wife and I once did a series of nighttime SCUBA dives. Darkness transformed the sea floor. We swept the tight circles of our flashlight beams across the muted coral, catching flashes of skittish nocturnal creatures.

As we ascended back toward the surface, the sea bottom melted into darkness. We made a decompression stop ten or twenty feet below the surface to let the nitrogen dissolve from our blood. There we hung, suspended in the void, with darkness stretching away on every side, above us, and below us. The sensory deprivation was absolute.

Panic welled up inside me. I could not tell if I was going up or down. I had no idea if I was even right side up. I felt like I was spinning. My eyes fixed on the stream of air bubbles from my own exhalation, the only indicator of orientation in this strange, spaceless world. Even with my wife beside me, I felt utterly alone.

The dark night of the soul feels much the same.

These times of profound disorientation are not pleasant, but they are gifts if we see them that way. If we don't know where we are going, our best course of action might be to sit still.

Sitting in stillness is uncomfortable in our go-go-go world but is essential to gaining self-mastery. Epictetus wrote, "The struggle is great, the task divine—to gain mastery, freedom, happiness, and tranquility." In his book *Stillness is the Key*, Ryan Holiday cites the journal of the late comedian Garry Schandling, who struggled with life pressures as he sought to find his own peace. Schandling writes, "To hold the mind still is an enormous discipline, one which must be faced with the greatest commitment of your life."[27]

Many people never find this stillness. They live on the run from themselves, hostage to rage and fear. They might have it together on the surface, but underneath is a tormented soul that does not know how to live in harmony with the world or itself.

When you sit alone in the wilderness, you find stillness, maybe for the first time in your life. You learn deep lessons about who you truly are. As you shed old identities, you open yourself to new ones.

St. John believed that the dark night of the soul, for all its sense of hopeless despair, was the path to union with God. Only when a soul was brought to a place of complete emptiness and dependence could it encounter divine light. In the dark night of the soul, we face the deepest and most elemental truth within ourselves. Annie Dillard writes:

> In the deeps are the violence and terror of which psychology has warned us. But if you ride these monsters deeper down, if you drop with them farther over the world's rim, you find what our sciences cannot locate or name, the substrate, the ocean or matrix or ether which buoys the rest, which gives goodness its power for good, and evil its power for evil, the unified field: our complex and inexplicable caring for each other, and for our life together here. This is given. It is not learned.[28]

Nothing about the wilderness experience can be rushed.

You might yearn to return to those green places where love and community and the day-to-day pleasures of life await, but the wilderness will not simply allow you to leave. It has things to teach, first.

The wilderness works its slow magic in you. In the forced stillness you discover peace. Your senses awake to a thousand small pleasures you would have overlooked anywhere else. Your restless spirit quiets down. Achievement loses its luster. You find that just by resting in a state of being, you make contact with forces so much deeper and more powerful than yourself.

The wilderness becomes enough.

You are ready to leave when you no longer care if you do.

PART FOUR

HEALING

HILL CLIMB

A few weeks after the fire, I hit rock bottom. I couldn't work. Uplift was dead in the water. I agreed to keep the organization alive, abruptly changed my mind, sent the order to dissolve, and then reversed myself again when my teammates protested. I had ceased leading effectively. My self-confidence was shattered.

One Sunday evening, we scheduled a board meeting to sort everything out. Before the meeting, to work off my debilitating stress, I went for a bike ride. I had never been the strongest or fastest cyclist, and a grueling ten-mile-long hill climb near my house had kicked my ass for the past year. I tried repeatedly but never made it all the way to the top.

This time, I decided I was tired of failure.

I would climb that goddamn hill if it killed me.

It took a long time, and I had to stop four times, but I did it. Two days later, I went back and did the entire thing without stopping. That hill never bothered me again.

I still had a long journey through failure ahead, but I'd like to think that was the day I started to get better.

BEGINNING

If recovery cannot be rushed, how do you begin?

That question became increasingly salient after my IT band injury. I could walk for miles but felt debilitating pain the moment I began to run.

My first thought, which seemed sensible, was to give the injury *time*. I stopped exercising for two weeks, then went for a short run. The pain returned immediately. I took a month off, then tried again. Same result.

If a month of rest could not heal me, I had no idea what to do. I feared I would never run again.

I finally visited my physical therapist, who told me I was doing it all wrong. A mile is too far, she said. Run for one minute, then walk and stretch for four minutes. Then do it again. And again. And again.

I obeyed but I felt ridiculous. My shortest "runs" took me over an hour and covered little more than a mile. My heart rate barely elevated. I must have provided great entertainment for the neighbors, running for such brief intervals and then stretching like I had just finished the Boston marathon.

This routine was boring and a little humiliating, but if this would get me better, so be it.

Before long I upped the running intervals to a minute and a half, then two minutes. I gradually shortened the recovery periods. At one point I ramped up too quickly, felt pain again, and backed off a little. I kept at it.

A month after I first visited my PT, I ran a hard 1.5 miles for my Air Force fitness test with no pain. Then I started piling on the distance: four miles, six miles, eight.

I had never been so happy to run in my life.

This physical recovery process gave me much to think about.

Physicians used to prescribe RICE for injured athletes: rest, ice, compression, and elevation. In recent years professional opinion has turned sharply against passive recovery. Physicians today prescribe *active recovery*.

Gentle movement of injuries promotes blood flow, facilitates the working of the lymphatic system, and helps ligaments and tendons heal. Exercise strengthens muscle tissue. Stretching extends range of motion and prevents further injury. Most sports medicine professionals today encourage athletes to remain as active as possible without aggravating an injury.

I suspect this holds a life lesson.

You have walked through failure. You have spent weeks or months in its gray drizzling aftermath, waiting for the sun to break through. You test yourself, try to run again, and realize you are still injured. It feels like you will never heal.

How do you begin to recover from that kind of weakness?

You cultivate strength over time.

As we have seen, failure can be a lengthy process, and your first responsibility is to walk that path with as much grace, dignity, wisdom, and shrewdness as you can. You can still reach better or worse outcomes. You must continue to fight for every last inch of success, or at least to stave off the very worst consequences of defeat. You will be weak during this season. You may be broken and bleeding, leaning on friends and family to carry you, barely able to sleep or get out of bed. But you do what you can.

And then, in quiet moments when you can begin to contemplate the future, you make yourself a promise: *no matter how long it takes, I will get strong again.*

As the worst fallout subsides, and you shed responsibilities, spaces open up in which you can begin to heal.

One way to start is by identifying your own equivalents of one-minute runs. You find micro-accomplishments that gently exercise the sore places, promote circulation, and build strength.

One-minute runs can be maddening. Because they are so small, they do not feel like victories. They may have nothing to do with the domains of life causing you pain, and yet they exercise the physical, mental, and emotional muscles necessary for healing.

For some people, that first one-minute run might simply be getting out of bed. Yes, there are days when the best thing you can do for yourself is sleep until afternoon. But unless you have a major illness, you are unlikely to heal by spending two weeks in bed. You must summon the strength to rise and face the day.

For other people, one-minute runs might entail carrying on with simple daily routines. At the end of brutal anxiety-inducing days, I often found solace in simple household chores. I felt satisfaction taking out the garbage, vacuuming the house, or making my bed. These are discrete tasks with beginnings and ends. They defy entropy and bring order to a disordered world. You can check them off a list. When you finish, you know you have accomplished something. Maybe the only thing you have accomplished all day.

"If you want to change the world, start off by making your bed," says Admiral William McRaven, a decorated SEAL and former commander of Joint Special Operations Command (JSOC). "If you make your bed every morning you will have accomplished the first task of the day. It will give you a small sense of pride, and it will encourage you to do another task and another and another."²⁹

Maybe you failed at writing or academics; the blank page leads you to dark places where demons lurk. Your one-minute run might be writing a paragraph or even a sentence.

Maybe your relationships are in disarray. You are wounded and hiding. When all your doubts and fears steer you towards isolation, your one-minute run might be picking up the phone to call a friend.

It might be accepting an invitation. Praying a few words. Stepping outside into the sunlight. Sending a query letter. Submitting an application.

Whatever it is, your one-minute run advances you a tentative step into an unknown future. You do this one thing and then you stop, rest, stretch, and assess yourself. Then you do it again and again. You learn to be okay with these small steps, and you know when to take your rests.

Before long, you can look back and see the miles accumulating behind you.

Then the realization dawns: you are moving again.

HEALTH

Failure invites us to renewed health.

Many of us view health as the absence of disease or injury, but this is only the beginning. Health entails physical, mental, and social well-being.[30] Healthy individuals are able to satisfy their needs, identify and realize their aspirations, and cope with change.[31] Health entails a dynamic sense of well-being that allows each of us to live at peace with our environment, the people around us, and even ourselves.

Health is, in many ways, the inverse of stress. We experience stress when our lives strain against the world instead of flowing with it. Stress occurs when we overexert our bodies, a marriage demeans our sense of personhood and autonomy, a job sucks away our soul, or our income fails to support our basic needs.

Health entails bringing the flow of our lives and our world into alignment. Sometimes this requires reordering our world, perhaps by seeking a new job or leaving an unhealthy relationship. But health often requires reordering ourselves. Health is partly something found within us, dependent both on how we treat ourselves and how we choose to receive what the world brings.

There is a balance here.

We should never resign ourselves to intolerable conditions. We must not shame the struggling, the depressed, or the broken by blaming them for their struggles or telling them to buck up.

Whenever we can, we should work for justice, fairness, and improvements in external conditions—both for ourselves and others.

At the same time, we cannot always change the world. Victor Frankl, despairing in a Nazi concentration camp, lacked the power to liberate himself. However, he knew he controlled his own attitude towards the events befalling him. That became the basis of his book *Man's Search for Meaning* and all his subsequent work.

Health entails confronting our anxieties, meeting our fears, and learning to hold our situation in our bodies without tension or sickness.

Health is not exclusively a matter of the body, but it must always include the body. Our bodies yearn to move, exert, and run. Healthy physicality energizes our souls and minds. Physical activity is how we move within the world, discover its treasures, and receive its gifts.

The aftermath of failure provides an opportunity to prioritize our health. We likely have unfilled time in our calendars. We are no longer too busy to exercise or too overwhelmed to step outside. We know that we have to treat our bodies with the respect they deserve if we are ever to get better.

Physical endeavors can also be a training ground for other aspects of our lives. My determination to climb Page Mill Road looks trivial in retrospect (any serious Palo Alto cyclist climbs it regularly) but remains a milestone in my life. It gave me a sense of accomplishment at a time I sorely needed it. That achievement also gave me a glimpse of how physical activity could help restore me to health and fortify other parts of my life.

For years my wife had urged me to try a triathlon. I had always pushed back. I didn't have time to train. I was a terrible swimmer.

Racing intimidated me. I was barreling towards a dissertation deadline and felt that every hour of my day needed to contribute to my academic success. After my failure, however, as I roamed Stanford's campus in a kind of daze, searching for ways to renew myself, I took a leap of faith.

I signed up for a swimming class. Three times each week, I stepped away from the hellish grind of academic uncertainty into bright sunlight and cold water. I worked muscles that had been dormant for years. My technique slowly improved. After each swim I felt the afterglow of endorphins and the pleasant ache of revitalized muscles.

I read articles on running faster, used a metronome to improve my cadence, and for the first time in my adult life made a deliberate effort to speed up my usual plodding pace. This was an exercise in taming fear, pushing my boundaries, and embracing pain in the name of self-improvement.

In late April I raced my first triathlon. The night before, as I arranged my gear, I felt like I was preparing for my execution. In the morning I kissed Wendy goodbye and rode the bus to the course start in grave silence. When the whistle blew, and I plunged into the cold lake, I realized almost immediately that two months of pool swimming had not prepared me for open water. I took off too fast. Someone kicked me in the face. Soon I was hyperventilating, unable to get enough breath. My freestyle devolved into a frantic dog paddle. Somehow I survived. The race was a blur after that: wind and sun on the bike, a hard run around the lake, a brief glimpse of Wendy and her triathlete friends cheering me on. I crossed the finish line, and a woman draped a finisher's medal around my neck.

My performance was nothing to write home about, but I had never felt so strong.

My friend John took up walking after Stanford suspended him for the second time due to incomplete work. He walked every day. He walked for miles. He walked in sun and he walked in rain. Each week, the pounds fell away. A kind of serenity dusted his life like snow.

For my friend Sam, it was hiking. Sam is one of the most brilliant people I know. He was so brilliant that he found his brief forays into college intolerable and never graduated, which made it difficult to launch a traditional career. With each passing year his hope of finding professional success grew fainter. He found his meaning and happiness in his lovely wife and beautiful son, along with his many creative talents, but eventually the bill came due; for years he has wrestled with the humbling challenge of providing for his family.

Sam set off into the hills. He had responsibilities, a family, and a time-intensive job. Scheduling every hike was a challenge and a sacrifice. But morning after morning he hit the trails, stretching himself to tackle ever-more difficult peaks in the Cascades. Strength and confidence flowed through him. We hiked together last summer, and I found myself struggling to keep up with his blistering pace through the shattered granite. He carries that strength into every other part of his life.

The power of physicality hit home for me during the Coronavirus lockdown. The strain overwhelmed our national psyche. We collectively realized that this would not end anytime soon. The economy faltered. People ran out of money and businesses closed. The fear and uncertainty were palpable, but throughout each day I saw dozens of people emerging into the sunlight, like survivors of a nuclear apocalypse crawling out of their underground bunkers.

I built a rock climbing wall in my driveway. Down the street, an older neighbor practiced martial arts in his front lawn. Other neighbors took up Tai Chi and yoga. Even in the midst of this global failure, we reached for health like a million green shoots growing towards sunlight.

Health is always a journey. It is never a destination.

We set noble intentions. Sometimes we fulfill them with discipline and determination. Other times we do not. Our health gets away from us, and we kick ourselves for our inconsistency.

Part of health is learning to be gracious with ourselves. The minute negativity intrudes, we are veering away from health. We are at war with ourselves again.

Life happens. That is part of the challenge.

After my first triathlon I had such wonderful intentions. I did a second, longer triathlon in the fall. I joined the Stanford triathlon team. I got stronger and faster than I ever had in my life. Then my dissertation fell apart, my world unraveled, and I stopped attending practices. I injured both my shoulders due to my lousy swimming form and will probably never swim any meaningful distance again.

John hit new challenges and stopped walking as much, at least for a time.

Sam faced new life pressures. The frequency of his hikes fell off, although he has been making a renewed effort lately, as much as his busy life allows.

They are doing their best. We all are.

We ride a cresting wave of personal growth, discover new kinds of success, and gather renewed strength. And then we zoom downward again with the waves breaking over us. It doesn't always feel like progress, but with each repetition, our internal resources grow stronger.

I tried to prioritize my health when I led Rogue Squadron. My team was strong and motivated, and we repeatedly hit home runs.

However, the stress was extraordinary, and I continually operated at my limits. My experience with Uplift had taught me to be careful and set strong boundaries. I paced myself for the long game. I vowed to never again burn out like I had before.

Even so.

One December afternoon, I felt ill and off-balance at work. When the symptoms abruptly worsened, I asked my friend Ryan to drive me to the Emergency Room. The next twenty minutes were a terrible blur. I lay curled up in the passenger seat of his Mustang, groaning against the worsening pain in my chest, while he muttered "Come on, come on!" and wove through traffic.

Preliminary tests at the ER suggested a pulmonary embolism. The doctors and nurses treated me with reverent concern. There was roughly a fifty-fifty chance that the blood clot would dislodge itself and I would die. I lay motionless in a hospital bed. I wrote a goodbye note to my family. I dearly hoped they would arrive before I died. When they did, I embraced them.

The final test came back: it was not an embolism.

To this day, we have no idea what happened that evening, but I still get sharp pains in that particular place in my chest whenever I am stressed. It feels like a piece of shrapnel, a ticking time bomb. I fear that if my stress ever crosses a certain threshold, I will set it off. I listen to my body whenever that pain flares up.

This abrupt threat to my health came as a shock, but I had been through failure and recovery before. I was getting the hang of this. I knew to take exquisite care of my body, no matter what.

The next week, I started training for my first marathon.

PLAY

As we grow older, too many of us forget how to play. We take ourselves far too seriously. The world demands too much of us.

This is a shame.

Play simply means attuning to the most creative and vital parts of ourselves. It means connecting with the raw joy and pleasure of being alive. Play lets our imaginations soar. Because we are not accountable for results, we can dream and dare without fear.

Who has time for that?

When you fail, you suddenly do have time. The world becomes a blank space, at least for a time, while you figure out what to do next. Play is also essential to healing; in the midst of this darkness, you have no choice except to do the things that bring you joy. Your life might depend on it.

Play helped me cope in the aftermath of the Stanford fire. For a year and a half, I had worked without ceasing. Other than time with my family, I had given almost every waking moment to my PhD studies and the Syria Airlift Project.

The day after the fire, I went hiking with friends and watched 4th of July fireworks. In the ensuing days I rose early in the morning, sat outside in the pre-dawn light, and watched birds and trees. I sketched pictures in a small notebook. I went to the library and flipped through architectural magazines, simply because that sounded pleasing in the moment. I went to the Stanford bookstore with no specific books in mind. I bought one book on creativity and another on physics. Neither had anything to do with drones or Political Science. I sat in the sun and read them.

It felt incredible.

In her memoir *The Sharp End of Life: A Mother's Story*, Dierdre Wolownick writes of her painful 23-year marriage coming to an end. As she puts the pieces of her life back together, she realizes how little she has ever done for herself. She has so much to learn about herself, relationships, community, and her own interests and passions. In this playful season she takes up marathon running to better relate to her daughter Stasia, and then rock climbing to better relate to her son, the legendary climber Alex Honnold, whose unroped climb of Yosemite Valley's 3,000 ft. El Capitan was captured in the film *Free Solo*.

Her book spoke to me precisely because Wolownick is not a superstar like her son. She is an ordinary mother, with no particular athletic talents, who laces up her sneakers for the first time in her mid-50s. She will never win an Olympic medal. She runs and climbs because these activities bring her joy and open up a dazzling new world of possibilities. They connect her to her children, new friends, and communities of people who find their lives enriched by their passions.

Wolownick will probably never become a professional climber, but at 66 she became the oldest woman to climb El Capitan. Her thirst to play also gave rise to her extraordinary memoir. Play gave her—and us—something far more compelling than a record marathon time or a mere climbing achievement. It gave us a story. It gave us *life*.

But see how seductive the lure of achievement is? I started writing about play with no rational payoff. Within paragraphs, I drifted into world records and revenue-generating books.

Play is rarely enough for us.

We demand more of it. Play is fine, we say, as long as it is a gateway into something more. Maybe it will be, and we can celebrate our good fortune. But often it isn't, and maybe that is the best kind.

Every parent fights this battle. We long for connection with our children, but every day a thousand distractions compete for our attention. Is it ever enough for us to watch our toddler descend the slide for the 37th time?

The utilitarian impulse cries out to do something more valuable. The phone is always in our pocket. We can watch our kids *and* send that e-mail or catch up with friends on social media or read the news. We can pop in our AirPods and consume an audiobook while still flipping cards in Candy Land; the kids will barely notice.

I am not picking on you; I am the worst about this.

We desperately resist giving ourselves over to frivolous play.

I am not sure why. Usually, when our children take us by the hand, they want to pull us into a world that is unbelievably fascinating, if we only have eyes to see. For children, everything is magical.

"Look at that cloud!" a daughter says. In that moment we have a choice. We can mumble a robotic, "Yes, honey, that's wonderful." Or we can look up and really *see* that cloud, and marvel at the shifting infinite variety in that vaulted sky, and imagine sailing ships and vast balloon-like elephants and dragons exhaling smoke.

We can hold roly-polys in our hand, catch ladybugs, build forts for ants, or craft swords from scrap wood and pretend we are knights. Having children gives us permission to revel in the world again.

We can still cultivate that childlike sense of wonder even if we do not have children. Wendy and I rented a beachfront condo for a portion of our honeymoon. When we arrived, I was aghast to discover that the balcony overlooked sprawling mud flats; we could barely see the ocean. I stalked angrily around the apartment for a while before I spotted Wendy lingering at the railing. When I joined her, I found that she was delighting in the innumerable species of birds and other creatures in the mud below—extraordinary little miracles of nature I had lacked the eyes to see.

All three of my children love to create. My son Isaiah went through a phase where he drew twenty or thirty pictures in a sitting. He stuffed every crevice in his bedroom with drawings, colorings, maps, mazes, stories, nonfiction books, songbooks, prayers, and handmade games. We literally could not keep up with him. Every few weeks I sneaked guiltily into his room with a garbage bag to cart off ninety percent of his work, snapping photos of the best and tucking the most precious treasures into a keepsakes box.

His creative output was staggering. I envied his disregard for anyone's opinion, least of all his own. He had no internal editor, no filter, no one to please... just the joy of unleashing that extraordinary imagination onto the page.

My children are each unique, and as they get older, their play changes. Isaiah built an elaborate website for a Hogwarts-style university that educates magic horses. Mariam loves to give gifts, and fills the world with cards, knitted scarves, and hand-made envelopes packed with treasures. Colin sews costumes and builds little houses for his stuffed animals, and is following in Isaiah's footsteps by building a website to teach chameleons how to hack computers. Last week all three built elaborate Viking shields out of scrap plywood. I scrambled to help when I heard them fire up the jigsaw.

This is play at its best. This is what we lose as we grow older and more responsible.

I mourn for what my children will lose. I want to stop it somehow, to take them by the shoulders and tell them how beautiful they are, how wonderful their imaginations are, warn them to never grow old.

But they will grow up. I cannot stop time.

Instead, I have to do something much harder: model what I want for them.

I have always wanted to learn to play the piano. During my final dissertation push, I finally tried. I needed an activity in which it was okay to be bad.

In the evenings after the kids went to bed, I poured a glass of wine, sat down at the piano, and hammered out crude renditions of musical masterpieces like *Mary Had a Little Lamb*, *When the Saints Go Marching In*, and *Jingle Bells*. I slowly built up a repertoire of chords.

So what if I played like an eight-year-old? I did it for myself. If I improved just a little each day, in two or three years I would be able to do what I have always dreamed of: sit down at a piano and fill silence with beauty.

Every missed note was a message to the world that I didn't really care what it thought, at least in this domain. It gave the finger to perfectionism, to the pressure-cooker of success and achievement. By engaging in an activity that had no utilitarian value, I reclaimed a tiny piece of my life.

I am embarrassed to admit these self-taught piano lessons did not last long. Life overran me. But that is okay, because this was play. Perhaps it was a bit like my children, pouring all their manic energy into building LEGO cities one week, sewing pillows the next, and then making chain mail armor the week after that. They love the thrill of discovery and learning. Play leads us to wherever we will be happy.

The Coronavirus lockdown reminded us of the importance of play at a national scale. Every individual, family, school, business, and government institution reached its breaking point. Each and every day, in new ways, we heard the thundering *crack* of strength encountering its limit. The damage was catastrophic, but somehow we are still here, struggling along, afraid, alone, reaching out, lifting each other up, trying to rebuild even as failures continues to unfold.

We have no choice except to yield ourselves to grace. To admit our limits, defeats, fears, and hopes. In the midst of all this, imprisoned within our own homes, play became an essential activity. Neighbors placed teddy bears in their windows to facilitate scavenger hunts for children. Families congregated on Zoom. We collectively devoured films and played board games online. Some of us tried to pick up another language or a musical instrument. Many of us struggled to get very far because we are stressed out and homeschooling and trying to work from home.

I took up piano again—for another two weeks. I made it a little further than before. I added Leonard Cohen's *Hallelujah* to my repertoire, a song that is at least beautiful.

We are trying. We haven't completely forgotten how to play.

That is good.

That is a beginning.

FRIENDSHIP

Shortly after resigning from Uplift, I began fulfilling a Teaching Assistant requirement at Stanford. One of my students was John, a thirty-year-old who was trying to bring closure to a chapter of his life by completing his undergraduate degree.

John was brilliant, articulate, and insightful. He had a gentle spirit and deep emotional intelligence, but for all his qualities, John also had an utter inability to complete written assignments. His terror of the blank page was like nothing I have ever seen. His personal demons had little to do with academic writing, but rather grew out of much deeper life experiences.

Stanford had already suspended John once because of his volume of incomplete work. He returned a decade later to give it another go.

I watched, helplessly, as John walked failure's path for a second time. He missed deadlines, was too ashamed to come to class, and broke promises to turn in his assignments late. Deep depression ensued. John's professors showed patience at first and made special accommodations, but every missed deadline wore out their goodwill. They could not comprehend his inability to complete his work. Their frustration became exasperation.

My own experience of failure had sensitized me. I knew what it was to be broken, to be taken past the limits of my strength. I understood the inability to answer simple emails. I knew how baffling this was to others. And I knew the embarrassment and shame that John must feel, the compounding debt of late work, the sense that others were losing faith in him.

I also knew that John was brilliant and talented and kind and gifted and that whatever hell he was going through right now, he would find life on the other side.

When Stanford finally suspended John a second time, I wrote him a note of encouragement and offered to meet for coffee. He accepted.

Because our relationship had been forged amidst John's crisis, we had no choice but to be our most vulnerable and authentic selves. John had nothing to hide. And in John, I found a kindred spirit who understood my own journey. I shared my experiences not to seek his sympathy, but to encourage him. That first conversation was cathartic for both of us. C.S. Lewis once wrote that friendship often begins with the exclamation, "What? You too? I thought I was the only one." Such was our experience.

In addition to our common experiences of failure, I learned that John was also a former Christian who could no longer embrace his childhood faith and—like me—had struggled to find community since then. Our journeys mirrored each other in so many ways.

I invited John over for dinner. Afterwards, we sat outside and watched the kids play and talked about storytelling and science fiction films and books we envisioned writing. John later came to watch Wendy's bike races and hosted board games for my children. Sometimes we kicked back, watched films, and analyzed the story and characters and cinematography.

In short, we became good friends.

One evening, some months later, we sat side by side at my dining room table, fingers clacking away on our respective laptops, brows furrowed in furious concentration. John was determined to clean up his incomplete grades. He needed to deliver three essays in the coming weeks. I suggested we write alongside each other.

Fifteen minutes. That was the deal. For fifteen minutes, both of us would do nothing but pour fresh words onto the page. No Internet surfing, no re-reading old work, no digging through dusty tomes for the perfect quote. We would write, write, write.

I was nervous at first that it wouldn't work. Only occasional clacks punctuated the long silence. I had some sense for the demons that prowled through his subconscious, and I knew they were howling in rage now. But he had promised to write, and I sat there next to him fulfilling my half of the bargain.

Amazingly, miraculously, magic seemed to be happening. The keystrokes rained down, sometimes light showers, sometimes torrents. I had no idea if the words would be any good, but that didn't matter. Many probably wouldn't be, but enough would.

This was John's one-minute run.

An essay was being born.

A heroic journey was unfolding.

A year later, Wendy and I were enduring some challenges in our marriage and I faced incredible stress at work. Life seemed to be falling apart. I had few close friends and hated troubling them with my problems; they had their own problems to deal with.

John was there for me. We went to coffee and I told him everything. John listened without judgment because he had *been there*. He knew how it felt to ride the careening waves of life, through all their ups and downs.

Any lingering power dynamic from our teacher-student relationship had disappeared. We were just two ordinary men doing the best we could in life, celebrating each other's successes and slinging an arm around each other's shoulders during the hard seasons. Neither of us could do much except listen, but that was enough.

Failure opens quiet spaces in our lives where true friendship grows. It demolishes pretenses and burns away the underbrush filling busy calendars. Relationships fueled by mutual benefit wither and die, but failure takes us to a liminal space where our deepest and most authentic selves yearn to connect. Something new and noble is being born, and it can only happen with the fellowship of other people.

Some of my richest moments of connection arose from this place of reemergence. Brian was my best friend in high school. I was Best Man in his wedding, and he in mine. Years later, when I was going through a crisis in my marriage, he was there to pull me back up.

We drifted apart in the years that followed. On a recent visit to Seattle, I reached out to him. I did not want to let this relationship atrophy.

We had dinner. Our children played. We laughed, reminisced, talked about old friends, and inventoried the interests and achievements of our children.

It was all... fine. Friendly. Sociable. But I felt like I did on my previous visits; the deepest essence of our friendship was missing. I had no idea how to rediscover it.

After dinner, while the children played downstairs, Brian's wife Leah alluded to a recent dark period in her life. When we gently inquired, she described starting a business, watching it fail, and falling into depression. Her failure had felt like a referendum on her abilities, competence, and identity. She had to grapple with foundational questions about who she was, where she was going, and what she wanted out of life. She came out stronger.

Brian talked next, about the rush of time and the sameness of his career after all these years. He thirsted to do something new and different with his talents as a videographer.

Then it was my turn. I had not told Brian and Leah about my religious deconstruction because Christianity had long been the basis of our friendship. I did not want to hurt them. I told them my story now, voice trembling. They met me with love and acceptance.

For an hour or so, our honest sharing about our deepest struggles brought us closer together than we had been in years. Each of us found the courage to show each other our truest selves. And each of us, in our unmasked glory, was beautiful and good.

I would like to think that failure has made me a better friend.

Many days, I am not sure. I am still solitary. I can be extremely selfish and am fiercely protective of my time. I do not let people get close easily.

Failure has softened me, however. I thirst to hear people's stories and understand the forces that have shaped their lives. I tire of many human foibles, but I rarely find such faults incomprehensible; by endowing me with a story of my own, failure has helped me to see the story in others.

The foundation of my moral framework these days is the Greek concept of *eudaimonia*, which means something like "human flourishing." I want that for myself and others. I want to listen, encourage, and help others grow to their fullest potential. That requires sensitivity to other people's stories, which is exactly what failure provides.

In 2017, after his ten-year hiatus from Stanford, John stood before a full auditorium as part of Stanford's Resilience Project and found the courage to share his story.[32] He told the audience, "They prepare you for everything here except for what to do when you fail." Then he lent his strength and wisdom to a room filled with young students each struggling with their own doubts, anxieties, and insecurities:

> There is no going back, but there is always a way forward… We are all alone, but we are all alone together. We each have a different journey, but we walk alongside. I'm still here. And you're here in this space with me. I am reaching out my hand to you, I am asking you to take it, and I am telling you: it will be okay. When your body is too heavy to get out of bed, it will be okay. When you are in the shower and your lungs breathe so fast that they cannot pull in air, it will be okay. When someone you love leaves you, now or forever, you will keep on living. It will be okay, because you're still here. And I'm still here. And as long as that's true, we'll all be okay.

I do not now where John's journey will lead him next, but I do know this: failure has made John an extraordinary friend. I hope others can say the same of me.

FAITH

Failure sets you on a journey of spiritual growth.

This begins in doubt, as we have already seen. But doubt is just the beginning.

For some, this journey will mean deepening within a particular religious tradition. These individuals wrestle with God, as Jacob did, confronting an apparent chasm between their beliefs and their lived experience. Their dark night of the soul leads to a new ability to rest in mystery.

For others, this might mean the adoption of new spiritual practices without necessarily adopting religious beliefs. Perhaps these individuals will look eastward to meditation, yoga, or the eightfold path.

For still others, this might be an entirely secular journey. If they use the word "spiritual" at all, it is only to refer to the soul's quest to understand its place in the universe.

Wherever you come down, failure summons you to new life.

I am not sure who I am anymore.

For whatever reason, between 35 and 40 years of age, almost every pillar of my life seemed to come crashing down. The collapse of Uplift Aeronautics became a symbol of what was happening inside my own soul. I outgrew the childhood faith that grounded my life, family, and community. My military career detoured into the wilderness. My venture into academia had not been the homecoming I expected. I lost the confidence of many people around me. The overarching theme of my professional life had been public service, but my time in the military coincided with a period of catastrophic U.S. foreign policy and chaos in the homeland.

I keep trying to reconstruct my life. I journal endlessly. In my free hours I tinker with this book, short stories that don't quite work, two half-written novels, academic journal articles, a memoir about innovation, a memoir about my religious transition, and a book on the evolution of political institutions. I flit between projects with manic intensity, struggling at all of them. It all looks so frantic and desperate. I know I'm *this close* to a meltdown.

Then I try to do the responsible thing and *step back*, and these days I spend so much time *stepping back* that I hardly do anything anymore. I want more than this. But what?

This is the darkest hour of my dark night of the soul.

The place I have absolutely nothing left.

When I was at my worst, I began experimenting with *vipassana* meditation. This involves relaxing the body and mind, focusing on the breath, and gently observing every transient thought originating within one's frantic, overactive mind. I imagined my thoughts as soap bubbles, rising up from within, popping as I spotted them.

A friend suggested envisioning myself as a mountain, permanent, unbending, while seasons and storms and earthquakes came and went. I found this meditation soothing and strengthening. It evoked my four years at the Air Force Academy, walking across the terrazzo at night, chilled to the bone, looking up through my crystallizing breath at the dark shape of Colorado's Front Range silhouetted against a wheeling expanse of stars.

In my darkest hour, I came up with my own meditation. I looked deep within myself for the one place untouched by the chaos. Deeper and deeper I went, until at last I arrived at the center: a crackling fire on a hilltop, surrounded by darkness. That fire was literally the only thing I could see in the darkness. It burned when all other lights had gone out.

When the stress and anxiety became intolerable, when a dark curtain veiled my future, I sat by that fire and watched the dancing flames. I retreated into the one place that could only be extinguished by death.

There is always such a place, if you can find it.

Gradually, you realize that this is not the end of the journey: it is a beginning.

When you leave that fireside, new life awaits.

Failure destroys certainties that should never have been certainties at all. You now understand how fragile and precarious and contingent everything is. The world offers no guaranteed recipe for success; anyone who says otherwise is selling snake oil. You can be the best in the world at your job, parenting, your sport, or your hobby, and one mistake or one day of bad luck can ruin you. Nobody is always right and nobody is always wrong, not even the Democratic or Republican party. Ambiguity is hard to live with, but if you can accept it, it liberates you.

Fear is the heart of fundamentalism. Fundamentalists crave certainty. The reason they cling so tightly to believing the earth is only 6,000 years old, or lead divisive church splinters over sprinkling or immersion, is because the slightest crack in canonized beliefs means the whole dam breaks.

This is not a Christian problem; it is a human problem. Fundamentalism courses through our blood. It is an instinct in almost every faith and every militant expression of non-faith. It lies at the heart of our corrosive political polarization.

Fear defined my religious life for almost two decades. I feared books on my shelves. I feared entire scientific disciplines. I feared people who differed from me and, with one wrong word, might further unravel my tattered faith. I feared disappointing loved ones.

Fear made my life into a living hell.

My life changed when I declared I was tired of being afraid. I would break those chains, even if it cost me every relationship and cast me into eternal flames. As I look back, I grieve that I lived so fearfully for so long.

We can go much deeper. Audrey Assad sings, "Out past the fear, doubt becomes wonder."

Failure drives you to deeper waters, like Moana sailing her outrigger canoe beyond the reef. With certainty gone, your spiritual journey becomes subtle and different. You soften. If you are a Christian, you become a better and wiser Christian. If you are a Muslim, you become a better and wiser Muslim. If you are an atheist, you become a better and wiser atheist. You retain an openness to mystery and surprise in an astonishing universe, and you see the lives of those around you as sources of profound insight.

Anxiety fades into a kind of peace. You discover that not knowing is okay. Maybe we would all be better off if more people knew as little as you.

I recently googled "overcoming disillusionment." A helpful commentator explained that disillusionment simply means "to be free from illusions." When you become disillusioned, you abandon a naive trust in things. You see the world as it actually is. Truth is never a bad thing.

Disillusionment has a second meaning: a "condition of being dissatisfied or defeated in expectation or hope."[33] That, I think, is the fate we need to avoid. Rising above despair is the heart of the spiritual quest.

I have been re-reading Anne Lamott lately. Anne is disillusioned in the first sense of the word but not the second. She knows firsthand the ugliness of the world, but she refuses to give up hope. Tragedy and beauty are intermingled in her world, and her starting place for authentic faith is acknowledging that we are all in this mess together.

In her book *Small Victories,* she quotes the poet Wendell Berry:

> it may be that when we no longer know what to do, we have come to our real work, and that when we no longer know which way to go, we have begun our real journey. The mind that is not baffled is not employed. The impeded stream is the one that sings.[34]

With so much in ruins, I keep feeling like I am at journey's end. But if Berry is right—and I think he is—maybe all of that was preparation. In my lostness and desperation, with absolutely nothing to say or offer the world, maybe the real journey is beginning. For now, maybe my experience of lostness is the most precious gift I can offer the world.

Maybe I am right where I need to be.

Gradually we must leave that fireside and re-enter the world. With our souls revitalized, we must look beyond ourselves to a world that needs what we have to offer.

Healing from failure drives us back to the basics of love, compassion, and kindness, which can never go wrong. After walking through our own dark valleys, we become attuned to the stories of those around us. We hear the silent cries for companionship, encouragement, and validation. We are prepared to answer.

My eight-year-old son is into skateboarding. Growing up as a strait-laced conservative, I thought of skateboarders as punks. My friend Eric urged me to look at them with new eyes. He recommended a documentary called *Bones Brigade*, which tells the story of boys like Tony Hawk, Lance Mountain, and Rodney Mullen who pulled together to form the best skateboarding team in history.

These men are in their fifties in the film, but as they look back, they quiver and cry and stammer as they describe abusive fathers, joyless childhoods, and lifelong complexes about their own inferiority. By the end of the movie, several of these grown men weep as they describe the beauty that lifted them out of their despair forty years before. Skateboarding was a conduit through which they experienced grace and belonging.

When we learn that Tony Hawk started a foundation to build skate parks in underdeveloped neighborhoods, we want to leap to our feet and shout, "Yes! Yes!" We see something holy at work. We will never judge those kids again. Each precious, punk soul is a battleground where eternal forces meet. If that is not authentic spirituality, I don't know what is.

And now we come full circle to the question of faith. We have lost so much along the way, but we have also found something new. We are learning to rest in the darkness, as Mother Theresa did, during those long decades when God fell silent. We open ourselves to others in ways we never could have imagined.

Oh, we will have our labels. We will have our beliefs, shifting and uncertain as they might be, but beneath it all we find the same bedrock: timid souls feeling their way home in the dark, helping each other along.

The small glimpses of beauty along the way, acts of kindness, and moments of connection are not merely grace notes in a grim symphony. They add up to something.

Even in our darkest hours, we find each other. We take each other's hands. Common values, common labors, and common dreams pull us together. New life arises in our communities. Acts of grace break forth at scale. We marvel as long-suffering activists achieve justice reforms, expand human rights, or tear down legacies of oppression. Acts of simple decency transfix the world. And these acts are everywhere.

That is the real story of our age: not government incompetence or a ravaging disease that defies all categorization or extreme polarization, but millions of small acts of daily kindness that hold our communities together when so much seems to be tearing us apart.

That is where I find my hope these days. More than ever, my faith is in the ordinary.

SCARS

Even as you heal, you discover that you will always carry scars.

You cannot endure something like this without changing forever. You learned what it is to feel helpless, overpowered by forces larger than yourself, unable to rise again for a time. Few people can walk away from that kind of experience unscathed.

I am mostly better now. The trauma from my season of failure largely passed. The aftershocks subsided to the occasional, faint rumble. I mostly feel strong again, and I meet the demands of each day with cool resolve.

At least, most days.

Some areas of my life remain tender to the touch.

I sometimes find myself in leadership situations that echo my worst experiences with Uplift. I experience these events like someone jamming a thumb into an open wound.

At one point, when Rogue Squadron was succeeding wildly, we were in a position to ask for nearly anything we wanted. Our team consisted of just three people, but my excited boss wanted me to ask for double-digit millions. I pushed back. Uplift taught me that growing too fast can be fatal. At this stage, that kind of money would have been like winning the lottery: it probably would have ruined our lives.

Our discussions became contentious. My baffled leadership could not comprehend why I was so opposed to shooting for the stars. I felt like a trapped animal, just as I had when Uplift was becoming overextended.

Angry, frustrated, and terrified of being trapped in a debacle, I sent a heated multi-paragraph email that damaged several key relationships. It also hurt my reputation in the organization, making me look volatile and unstable. The fallout threw me into an emotional tailspin, shattered my self-confidence, and left me questioning my ability to work in an entrepreneurial organization.

I learned that one of my scars is an abiding terror of overcommitment.

My problem is that I am too excitable, too passionate, too quick to find faults in the status quo and suggest improvements. If someone brings me a problem, I spin up like a warp core. I talk animatedly. I gesticulate with my hands. I scribble diagrams on whiteboards. I write white papers in single, manic afternoons. I suggest idea after idea to do things better.

Days or weeks later, I discover that colleagues expect me to take ownership of executing all these grand ideas, which was never my intent.

At this point, I panic.

I don't have time, I tell them. I'm overextended.

Then everything unravels. My colleagues get angry because I gave so many signals that I was committed to this. They are trying to help me, they say. And I get guilty and awkward because I know they are partly right, that I probably had implied a personal commitment, even though I thought I had been clear about my limits. Now the whole thing is a muddled mess, and everyone is angry with each other.

I am especially terrified of owning responsibility for efforts I believe will fail. Unfortunately, this happens to me somewhat regularly because I am most likely to speak up when I believe something is about to go off the rails. Somehow, that approach often ends with me being placed in charge.

I never learn.

When I feel overcommitted, I get mean and nasty. I fight like a caged animal. My emotions go off the charts. I vacillate between soaring optimism about new possibilities and stalking, raging, mumbling fits. In these moments, my coworkers probably think I am a mental case and an ass.

Later, alone with my thoughts, I wonder why I am such a mess.

The answer is clear: I have been trapped in failure before. I know what it's like to feel that crushing weight on my back for month after endless month, unable to breathe, and unable to escape. I never want to be in that place again.

So when danger appears, my amygdala floods my brain with fight-or-flight chemicals, jolts with me with adrenaline, spikes my heart rate, and tenses every muscle. The same instincts that evolved to protect me from ravenous lions in the African savannah urge me to escape with my life.

My poor, faithful body. It is doing everything in its power to protect me.

After you fail, you will carry your own scars. Every person's will look different. You might never want to talk about some topics again, just as you might have a lifelong aversion after a bad case of food poisoning. You might carry lifelong fears of particular people, places, or types of situations. Your inventory of inner strengths and weaknesses may forever look different. For the rest of your life, you will view the world through the lens of your failure, guided by powerful intuitions that can serve and protect you.

Your intuition in these cases will often be right.

Behavioral scientists tell us that expertise is largely a matter of pattern recognition. We hear stories of firefighters who are overcome by a sudden sense of calamity. They can't explain it, but they escape the burning house moments before a fireball erupts. A good pilot is attuned to every hum and vibration in the cockpit; his body registers the slightest deviation, and he knows immediately that something is wrong. Decades of experience are etched into the brains and bodies of these experts, allowing them to make accurate judgments without conscious thought.

The trauma of failure is not so different.

Every scar inscribes knowledge in your body. You know what it is to be hurt, trapped, broken, or humiliated. You have a sixth sense for danger. You are a bit like Frodo now; every time the Ring-Wraiths drew near, he felt searing pain in his chest where the Witch-King of Angmar had once stabbed him with a cursed blade.

When you carry wounds like this, you might not always be the life of the party. But as you stand in the shadows with your drink in hand, and look out over this sea of young people with their bright eyes and endless optimism about how everything is going so swimmingly, you feel set apart.

They have so much to learn.

You have the benefit of hard-won wisdom.

On the other hand, your intuition can sometimes be wrong. Our worst failures scorch traumatic experiences into our nervous systems. We might be hypersensitive for the rest of our lives. We might jump at shadows. Our nervous systems might desperately fight to protect us from threats that no longer exist.

My intuition generally serves me well these days, helping me to identify threats and find my way through complex and dangerous situations. On the other hand, it can also make me overly cautious.

I owe most of my achievements to partners who pushed me to take big leaps into the unknown. In each case they pushed for decisions that I thought were too ambitious, fast, or reckless. I freaked out. I got mean. I lost my cool with friends and colleagues who were trying to help me, who owed me nothing, who had every right to walk away. Instead, they put up with me. We launched new efforts, and we saw results I never could have achieved alone.

The truth is, I am wrong nearly as often as I am right.

This has given me a healthy fear of myself. Despite my best efforts to remain open to the world and supple in my perspectives, I am calcifying into a fossil of my lived experience. It happens to all of us. I respect my intuitions but also fret over them. I am never sure if they are working for me or against me.

Time heals, but it rarely heals everything, so you learn to manage your wounds. You learn to show your face again, even with all that scar tissue.

You develop a realistic understanding of your limits and boundaries. You know how hard you can work before flaming out. You know what triggers you. You become acquainted with your personal version of Mr. Hyde, the brutish thing you become when you are cornered and the flashbacks come.

You realize the importance of working with others. Your friends and colleagues have scars of their own, but they are different from yours. There is goodness in that, because you can carry each other when old injuries get the better of you. Your fellow travelers can tell you when you are being prudent and when you are being unreasonable. The answer may not always be clear, but you will at least have additional perspective. Somehow, you will push through.

WAITING

One day it occurs to you that you are finally getting better.
You are sleeping through the night again. Your one-minute runs have become two-minute runs and eventually 5ks. You have discovered who your real friends are and have reveled in renewing those relationships. You have indulged in long-forgotten hobbies, relaxed with favorite novels or movies, and spent entire weeks doing nothing at all. From time to time you feel the tremor of aftershocks, but you take them in stride. You learn to live with your scars.
Although you have enjoyed this time of rest and healing, you feel restless. You long to challenge yourself, to apply your energy and talents to something that will provide meaning and purpose. You yearn to create, build, learn, compete, explore, or dare.
But what does that even mean?

Your old life is gone. Nothing anchors you to any particular future or tells you which way to go. The sheer scope of possibilities unnerves you. This open-endedness is a problem you never anticipated.
Psychologists have invented a variety of terms to describe this dilemma. Barry Schwartz calls it the paradox of choice. He writes that an abundance of choice "can make you question the decisions you make before you even make them, it can set you up for unrealistically high expectations, and it can make you blame

yourself for any and all failures."[35] When faced with too many options, we fall into decision paralysis.

Even when you have a sense of direction, there is no telling when you will find your next opportunity. You might spend months looking for a new job before you get a nibble. The dating scene might appear hopeless. You might resolve to be a better parent, but it will be weeks before your teenager even wants to speak with you. You might bounce from failure to failure for years before something finally connects.

This ambiguity about the future is one of failure's last, unexpected cruelties. Right when you are feeling better and have every reason to be optimistic, you can fall into a psychological abyss.

Waiting can be one of your hardest challenges yet.

I have been doing a lot of waiting lately.

A few months ago, my involvement with Rogue Squadron came to an abrupt, traumatic, and unexpected end—a story I will tell later.

For the previous two years I had worked nonstop, burdened with responsibilities, always on the verge of burnout. Almost overnight, all that weight was lifted from my shoulders. Furthermore, my removal coincided with the beginning of a Coronavirus shelter-in-place order. I was suddenly home all day, every day, with very little responsibility. My next military assignment—as a professor at SAASS—would not begin for four months.

Losing my role in Rogue Squadron was devastating but I also felt an exhilarating sense of possibility. I resolved to look to the future. With all this time and energy, I could do whatever I wanted, become anything. I could experiment with new identities, at least for a while, until I settled into my next thing.

This season of waiting was exhilarating—for a while.

Over time, the anxiety came roaring back. I had no direction. I struggled to use all those glorious, empty hours. I flitted from project to project, unsure whether I should be a fiction writer or a freelance coder or an innovation consultant or an academic. I second-guessed myself every time I began something.

No one would ever hire me as a software developer, I concluded; I'm too old, and even if I did get hired, I'd earn starter wages. Same thing with academic work. Government innovation made me miserable, so why would I even think of being a consultant? My fiction was pure garbage, and there was no money in fiction anyway unless you are J.K. Rowling or can roll a new romance novel off the assembly line every month.

Thinking about money made me panic, and then I stopped working on my creative project of the moment in order to review my budget for the ten thousandth time. I worried about what would happen when I retired from the military in a few years. I had dark visions of being a washed-up Colonel with no skills and a too-big mortgage who drifted from dead-end job to dead-end job and spent his retirement hanging out at the shopping exchange on the nearest military base.

I have been through failure before.

I am learning how to manage myself.

Around the time I get to the washed-up Colonel part, I put down my project and go sit outside with a cup of coffee. I watch black squirrels scamper across power lines. I look at flowers. Every afternoon a fat yellow bird with a wandering eye that I call Dopey flits into my yard to peck at the seeds my kids spilled while filling our bird feeder. Sooner or later, a vicious blue bird that has become the bane of my quarantine existence screeches in and drives Dopey off in a frightened flurry of wings. Some days I throw shoes at

Blue Bird.

I sit there in the grass, barefoot, drinking my coffee, and let the goodness of the day wash over me. I give myself permission to wait. I joke, somewhat seriously, that I am going to be a very good elderly person.

All of us find ourselves here sooner or later.

Everyone's waiting place looks different.

My wife Wendy is a committed athlete. She used to compete in triathlons, until a lingering hip injury made it too painful to run. After that, she switched to racing bikes. During the season when I was building Rogue Squadron, she joined and later helped run a women's bike racing team.

As we prepared to move away from California, Wendy did one final gravel bike ride with two close friends. The day went to hell, and by afternoon a catastrophic chain of events was unfolding. Wendy and her friends found themselves stuck on a remote ridge, facing unexpectedly difficult terrain, under searing afternoon heat, and out of water. Tired, stressed, and dehydrated, Wendy fell hard. The result was an open fracture in her elbow, a dramatic helicopter extraction, and two surgeries.

As I write, Wendy is waiting.

Her right arm is still splinted and nearly useless. It will be weeks or months before she can ride a stationary bike, let alone a real one. Before, she fell into negative emotional spirals if she missed a single workout. Now it is all she can do to take walks around our yard or neighborhood.

We have no idea what the future will bring. I do know that Wendy will ride again, literally or metaphorically. Nothing can hold her down.

But in the meantime, she must wait.

When you are ready to get on with your life again but find yourself trapped in this waiting place, all you can do is keep showing up. You need a certain amount of luck, but as the old saying goes, luck is what happens when opportunity meets preparation. You keep playing. You keep exploring. Sooner or later, goodness happens.

In the meantime, you keep taking care of yourself. You are still a bit fragile, still healing. You might be for the rest of your life. You recognize that getting back on your feet will take time and the process can't be rushed. You will not solve all your problems today. You need not chart a course for the rest of your life.

So when suffocating anxiety squeezes your chest, or you have nightmares about being lost in a broken-down car, you give yourself a break. You rub your eyes and get up from your desk. You breathe. You meditate. You call a friend or drink tea with your spouse or wrestle with the kids. You go for a walk, look at flowers, and watch the birds.

You keep showing up for life.

Most days, that is enough.

Sooner or later, life will begin again.

PART FIVE

RENEWAL

REINVENTION

The reason you got to this place—broken, burned out, defeated—is because something in your life no longer worked for you. Your startup idea was not good enough. You made irrecoverable leadership mistakes. You were miserable with a spouse you probably never should have married to begin with. Your book manuscript was unsalvageable, no matter how many months you spent polishing. Your impostor syndrome made every single day of your PhD experience a torment, and you realized in the end that you didn't even like the work. You hated your job but were afraid to move on.

And now, here you are.

Whatever went so badly in your life, it is over now.

You are free from all that weight of expectation, whether imposed by you or others.

The sense of relief can be indescribable.

You feel a sense of *lightness*.

Of possibility.

Of being someone new.

"From childhood to old age, there is hardly a moment when one is not confronted by scripted life," Gabriel Rockhill writes.[36] Family and society bombard us with messages about who we should be, the roles we should play, and the principles we should embody. These scripts are often invisible, insidious, and so deeply internalized that we cannot even see them.

When failure strikes, we realize the old script never completely worked for us. Despite our best efforts to play the part, something was amiss. We denied it or concealed it, but now the incontrovertible evidence lies before us.

James Hollis, a Jungian therapist, teaches that anxiety and discontent are not mere pathologies; they are cries from deep within our subconscious, pleading with us to pay attention to something out of balance within the soul.

Failure forces us to acknowledge that who we are, and what we want out of life, is different than we once thought. Diana Glouberman writes that when our heart and soul go out of something, we need to "stop, acknowledge our feelings and the outer realities, find our truth and follow it. In other words, we need to live truthfully."[37]

We have no more excuses. Our previous life disappeared or at least permanently changed. Our responsibilities are temporarily lessened. We have the opportunity to let something new grow.

"Cracks in the foundations of our life narratives can have the surprising effect of clearing space for unforeseeable developments," Rockhill continues. "Like the seeds that sprout in toxic soil, or push up through slabs of oppressive concrete, re-emergence and reinvention become possible."

Barbara Bradley Hagerty, in a book about finding purpose and joy in midlife, expresses a similar message.[38]

> Part of midlife's challenge is to closely examine the old script— the one that family and society writes for you, the one in which you are meeting everyone else's expectations— and see if it needs revision. The new script is tailored to your core identity— your own talents, passions, and personality— and these should

shape your goals. For some, this means a major revision, bringing in a new cast of characters and an entirely new location. For others, it means rechanneling one's energies just a few degrees into something that gives them meaning and verve.

The aftermath of failure gives you space to become who you really are.

As we put our lives back together, it is easy to focus on the externals. We ask ourselves whether we need a career change, what hobbies we should pursue, or which friends we should spend time with.

These are all important, but reinvention goes much deeper. Reinvention is about discovering who you *are*.

Franciscan Friar Richard Rohr writes about "first-half-of-life" and "second-half-of-life" concerns.[39] David Brooks uses the metaphor of two mountains.[40] For both authors, reinvention brings a fundamental transformation of values. The first mountain is about achieving personal ambitions, dreams, and goals. During their hustling years on that mountain, people fret over reputations and ego satisfaction. They strive for excellence and self-improvement in order to find happiness and fulfillment.

Then the valley happens. The failures. Lost jobs, illnesses, scandals, divorce, estrangement, the deaths of loved ones, the crises of meaning and purpose. Those in the valley find themselves suffering and adrift. They are called to a new expedition.

Not everyone accepts the invitation. In this season of crisis, some people retrench into who they were. David Brooks writes that these people "seem to get smaller and more afraid, and never recover. They get angry, resentful and tribal."

Other people find their way out of the valley to a second mountain—a life of spiritual richness, close relationships, generous service, and sensitivity "to the joys and pains of the world." We know these people when we meet them. They seem almost incandescent, radiating peace and quiet joy. Laughter has left its indelible imprint in the soft lines of their faces. Life experience broke something in them, and in doing so, set them free. Their world is evergreen.

Mr. Rogers springs to mind. So does my Uncle Doug, who shared a similar temperament. He spent a successful career in the electronics industry, but if you spoke to him any time in the past thirty years, you would never know that. Instead, he would tell you about his cherished group of friends who meet every Tuesday morning. He would guide you to his porch and show you the rock garden a friend arranged for him beside the creek. He would point out every animal within sight of his tiny townhouse. He would tell you about his latest walk, the joys of cycling well into his 80s, and the latest presidential biography he had read. Tears would spring to his eyes as he spoke about gratitude.

Uncle Doug's transformation was not merely from a hard-working professional into a pleasant retiree. Somewhere in those years, he underwent a profound personal transformation. Decades of reflection, friendship, reading, and a practiced discipline of gratitude had shaped him into a modern saint.

Reinventing yourself can be intimidating.

No one directs your life anymore. That sacred responsibility belongs to you. As childhood scripts lose their power over you, the world becomes unimaginably vast.

When I felt called beyond the safe harbor of my childhood beliefs, I panicked. I told my pastor that I felt like I was casting out to sea on a flimsy raft.

As I began to explore my freedom, the metaphor changed. My life was not a raft; it was a sailing ship, strong and seaworthy, and I was embarking on an extraordinary voyage. I could go anywhere I wished in this vast archipelago of life. I was free to set anchor in a quiet Buddhist cove one morning, even if I had no intent to stay, then set sail to learn about 21st century neuroscience or evolutionary biology the next. I could spend weeks fishing and watching sunsets with a circle of friends on one island, then welcome students aboard to sweep them off on a tour of exotic coral reefs. I could still visit the safe harbor of my childhood beliefs whenever I wished and could furnish my ship with my favorite possessions from those familiar lands.

Sailing the ship of life is a great responsibility. There are sandbars, whirlpools, and rocky outcroppings that can smash a ship to bits. You must sail with wisdom and prudence. You must keep your ship in good repair. A good ship needs a crew, as it is dangerous to sail alone. You face many challenges when you leave harbor, yet anyone who has tasted the salty air and felt the sea spray on their face knows that the journey is worth it.

As a Christian, I loved the writings and worldview of C.S. Lewis. I once kept a personal blog titled *Into the Utter East*, which derived its name from the noble promise of Sir Reepicheep the Mouse as he sails east across Narnian seas. He tells the crew:

> My own plans are made. While I can, I sail east in the Dawn Treader. When she fails me, I paddle east in my coracle. When she sinks, I shall swim east with my four paws. And when I can swim no longer, if I have not reached Aslan's country, or shot over the edge of the world into some vast cataract, I shall sink with my nose to the sunrise.[41]

Many years later, having outgrown a script that never well suited me, this quote still means as much to me as ever. I have sailed longer and farther than I ever dreamed possible. I have known many storms, been shipwrecked more than once, and lost many things precious to me. But I have also known glories and wonders that I would not trade for the world. The work of reinvention goes on. I sail ever onward in pursuit of goodness, truth, and beauty.

Your journey will look different from mine, but also not so different.

We will both press on into the great unknown.

Into the utter east.

FREEDOM

When you fail, you learn just how little control you have over your life. You could be brilliant, talented, ambitious, rich, famous, successful—and tomorrow you could be in handcuffs or diagnosed with terminal cancer.

Fame is fleeting. You could start ten successful companies or write ten brilliant novels, and the eleventh might be a spectacular failure. Do hard things long enough, and failure is all but guaranteed. When that happens, you discover that the fickle mob loves to eat its former heroes alive. Latent within admiration are jealousy and contempt.

In summary, failure teaches you the cyclical, ephemeral nature of success. Ryan Holiday writes that we are always in one of three states: aspiring, succeeding, or failing.[42] Life turns like a wheel.

We bristle at this claim.

We will be different.

Life eventually puts us in our place. Sooner or later, we have to admit that Holiday is right. Once we stop resisting and accept the cyclical nature of success and failure, we discover an unexpected blessing: freedom.

During my recovery from Uplift, I discovered Stoicism, a practical life philosophy that is essentially an extended application of the Serenity prayer attributed to Reinhold Niebuhr: "God grant me the serenity to accept the things I cannot change; courage to change the things I can; and wisdom to know the difference."

Stoicism teaches us to flow with the world. The Greek Stoic philosopher Epictetus wrote:

> Make the best use of what is in your power, and take the rest as it happens. Some things are up to us and some things are not up to us. Our opinions are up to us, and our impulses, desires, aversions—in short, whatever is our own doing. Our bodies are not up to us, nor are our possessions, our reputations, or our public offices, or, that is, whatever is not our own doing.[43]

In other words, Stoicism provides a framework for flourishing in a world that vacillates endlessly between triumphs and defeats. It teaches us to make peace with forces larger than ourselves.

We cannot always change the world, but we can change ourselves.

Some say Stoicism is too defeatist. They think it means giving up on the world, surrendering our ambition, or settling for defeats instead of fighting hard for victories.

That is not the point.

The greatest Stoics were not passive bystanders; they were men of the world who used their power to shape history. Emperor Marcus Aurelius led the Roman Empire through numerous wars and a plague that killed five million people. Marcus suffered. He knew better than anyone the limits of his own power. Enemies besieged him. His health suffered and he wrestled with insomnia. We can imagine him scribbling his famous *Meditations* as a way to soothe his own nerves. He passed his Empire and all his achievements to a disappointing and unstable son who, in the words of one contemporary, turned Rome's history "from a kingdom of gold to one of iron and rust."[44] Despite all that,

Marcus continued ruling as best he could.

Seneca, another famous Stoic, was a dramatist and statesman who tutored the Emperor Nero. His professional success turned to a nightmare as Nero became increasingly deranged. According to Tacitus, Seneca tried to retire twice but Nero refused him. As much as possible, Seneca retreated from the court to his country estate and his writing. One can only imagine Seneca's agony, watching Nero drive his beloved Rome to ruin, taking his own reputation with it. Nero eventually accused Seneca of complicity in an assassination plot and ordered Seneca to kill himself. This great statesman of Rome met his end in a bathtub with his veins open.

Marcus Aurelius and Seneca lived in the real world. They were ambitious change makers. They put on their sandals each morning, gave speeches, wrote treatises, led people, fought political battles, and suffered at the hands of their enemies.

However, they were also philosophers who recognized how much lay beyond their control. They could let that knowledge destroy them, or they could master themselves. They believed that suffering came not from the hard events of their lives, but from their subjective experience of those events.

Marcus and Seneca leveraged philosophy to transform their subjective experience of the world. Even as they marshaled their powers to steer history, they found peace in flowing with the world. Stoicism gave them inner freedom, no matter the circumstances.

As I prepared for my dissertation defense, my anxiety was crippling.

I had no idea how my committee would view my work. I might receive accolades and quick signatures. Then again, I might face an interrogation about the myriad ways my work fell short. I might spend the next three months tearing my abomination of a dissertation down to its foundation and starting over. I had to be prepared for either possibility.

I ruminated on the anger, hurt, and sense of injustice I would feel if the committee pronounced failure. I imagined delivering a speech about the ways I felt unsupported, the casual rejection of work I had invested hundreds of hours in, the walls I encountered when I tried working outside conventional norms. I would stand before my inquisitors like Martin Luther, shining with courage and determination. *Here I stand; I can do no other.*

Over time, I realized this fantasy was not just unwise but represented destructive mental framing. Righteous indignation was precisely the wrong response to a committee of leading scholars who pushed me to become my best possible self.

They were not perfect advisors; at times, they had inadvertently hurt and frustrated me. But they always meant well, and invested great time and energy in helping me cross the finish line. If they deemed my dissertation not ready, it was for precisely one reason: it was not ready. They would be saving me from mediocrity. The proper response—the Stoic response—would be gratitude for mentorship under luminaries in my field, who insisted on nothing less than excellence.

I revised my imaginary speech. If I failed, I would apologize for falling short of their expectations, thank them for pushing me to excellence, and promise to return with better work the next time around.

That reframing brought a cool sense of relief.

Whether I passed or failed, I would grow and improve. Of course, I desperately wanted to pass, but once I accepted the possibility of failure, my burden became more tolerable.

As it was, I passed. I felt like a rock star. I felt so confident, in fact, that I tried to write an additional chapter afterwards, only to meet my advisor's strong disapproval. He probably felt like he was reeling in a kite in a thunderstorm. Chastened, I tamped down my enthusiasm and dutifully completed the required revisions.

A few months later, a not-very-good journal invited me to write a piece for a special issue. I figured this would be an easy win, so I spent a month writing the article. The journal awkwardly rejected it.

The dance of success and failure goes on and on. Once you understand that, you can stop worrying so much.

Before, you were clinging white-knuckled to the edge of your success, desperate to hang on. One false move could undo everything.

After your failure, you realize you were doomed from the beginning. I mean that in the nicest possible way. There was *always* going to be a plunge in sales, a social media firestorm, a painful fight, a closed door, or a sick child who makes all your material success look insignificant. It was just a question of when and in what form.

Every executive is sweating right now. Good heavens; this is not the message we want our investors and managers and employees to take away. We need to instill confidence, swagger, a vision of infinite possibility. Surely this kind of fatalism will undermine our future success.

Or will it?

In 2018 Amazon.com CEO Jeff Bezos told his employees, "One day, Amazon will fail. Amazon will go bankrupt." Their job was to focus on customers and "try and delay that day as long as possible."[45] Whatever you think of Amazon or Bezos, good on him for having the intestinal fortitude to tell the truth. His speech was like telling a room full of anxious, hand-wringing homo sapiens that each and every one of them will die someday. Of course they will. Now that we have that out of the way, we can get on with the business of living.

Once you accept the wave-like regularity of success and failure, you can ask the right questions and plan for the right futures.

Life was never about chasing success or running from failure.

Of course you should always give your best and aim for success, but fortune changes like the weather. Far more important than the conditions on any given day is your own attitude. Consistency emerges from how you perceive the world and live in relationship with others. If you are a leader, you guide other people on their own journeys as well.

The irony is that finding this inner freedom provides your best chance at success. Sun Tzu tells us, "the general who wins a battle makes many calculations in his temple ere the battle is fought."[46] I cherish this image of a general kneeling before his ancestors in a place of peace and sanctuary, finding his own center before stepping into battle. For Sun Tzu, the skillful general is temperate and self-controlled, not ruled by passionate emotions.

Professional athletes understand that peak performance requires transcending worry and fear. A gold medal performance requires focused attention, calm, and an almost graceful flow with the world. Fear undermines the conditions necessary for success.

If you can find this inner calm in the face of success or failure, then no matter who you are or what your circumstances, you will always breathe free air. That freedom comes from within you. Nobody can ever take it away.

COURAGE

Failure has a curious side effect.

Even though it devastates your self-confidence in the short term, it imprints much deeper confidence in the long term.

Before, failure was something abstract and terrible. It circled ominously in the sky above you, felt but not seen. You tossed and turned at night, terrified of all the ways it might strike.

And then your worst fears were realized. Failure sank its talons in you. Its putrid smell filled your nostrils. Flesh tore, bones broke, your spirit groaned. And then the evil thing passed, one final shadow blotting out the sun before it vanished towards the horizon, leaving you alone in the harsh desert light.

Failure did its worst, and you are still here.

Uncertainty is the heart of fear. We live in terror of what we do not know or understand. When we survive failure's attack, we gain knowledge. We emerge wiser, shrewder, battle-hardened.

No two episodes of failure will ever be quite the same, but at least we know the shape of the thing, the feel of the attack, and each intimate stage of its assault. If we handled it this time, we can handle it next time.

Failure gives us courage.

We are no longer afraid of failure.

At least, not like before.

Leading Rogue Squadron was the most stressful job I have ever had. I never knew when or where failure might strike. I felt like those doomed space marines in *Aliens*, creeping through corridors and sweeping their rifle-mounted flashlights over wet, glistening things in the dark. They hear scuttling in the vents, glimpse faint shapes through the steam, see horrific traces that their adversary has been there ahead of them. An ambush could lie around any corner.

New threats assaulted Rogue Squadron every day. Entrenched incumbents shut us out of meetings and outmaneuvered us in conference rooms across Washington D.C. Rival organizations stole code. Millions of dollars of expected funding disappeared without a trace in the swamp of Congressional gridlock, continuing resolutions, and broken government processes. IT constantly tried to shut down needed software development tools. Government abused our people—tampering with salaries, imposing undue restrictions, failing to follow through on promises, dragging its feet on contract negotiations to keep my team employed. We always risked losing our best talent.

I agonized over all the ways failure could strike. A security breach. A disgruntled employee sabotaging our network. A spiral of technical debt that ground our software development cadence to a halt. DoD passing some new regulation that instantly made our software off-limits to troops. My journals are a shrine to my anxiety and paranoia. But as the old saying goes, it isn't paranoia if they really are out to get you.

Facing constant threats, amidst so much uncertainty, is a ruthless mind game. Unfortunately, this is a common state of affairs for anybody who dares to lead people, build something, commit to a relationship, have children, or drive social change. The practical challenges you will face are nothing compared to the challenge of managing your own mental health.

Ben Horowitz, author and cofounder of the venture capital firm Andreessen Horowitz, writes:

> By far the most difficult skill for me to learn as CEO was the ability to manage my own psychology. Organizational design, process design, metrics, hiring and firing were all relatively straightforward skills to master compared to keeping my mind in check. Over the years, I've spoken to hundreds of CEOs all with the same experience. Nonetheless, very few people talk about it and I have never read anything on the topic. It's like the fight club of management: The first rule of the CEO psychological meltdown is don't talk about the psychological meltdown.[47]

It takes courage to show up every day, knowing this is what you will face.

You will have good days when the team is on fire, the product delivering, the customers delighted. Many evenings you will sit hand-in-hand with your spouse, glowing with affection, overwhelmed with gratitude. On hot summer days you will feel transcendent joy as you watch your children leap through the sprinkler.

However, you will also feel the existential dread of knowing that this moment cannot last. You will sense some faceless threat lurking on the horizon, ready to swoop in and ruin everything. Even when all seems well, you will find it hard to trust goodness.

So you must manage yourself.

There is only one way to learn how to survive in the arena: fight in the arena.

You can read books and listen to podcasts. You can speak with hardened warriors who went before you. You can walk the battlefield some quiet evening, familiarize yourself with the terrain, and imagine what this place will look like when transformed by daylight and crowds roaring for blood. But in the end, nothing can fully prepare you to watch that iron gate rising, to see the bright sunlight spilling into your pen, to know that nothing now separates you from an enemy whose sole thought is eviscerating you.

Modern military forces understand this. We have a principle: *train like you fight*. Fighter pilots in Vietnam had much longer life expectancies if they survived their first five combat missions; that trial by fire gave them the experience, steeled nerves, and quiet confidence to prevail in combat. That led the Air Force to develop realistic, scenario-based training.

As an Air Force pilot, I experienced this principle firsthand. Every graduate of the U.S. Air Force Academy remembers the silent terror of riding the blue bus towards the first moments of basic training. I felt echoes of that experience years later, when a similar bus swept me off to a three-day confinement in a simulated Prisoner of War camp. There I spent a long night crammed in a pitch-black cell the size of a closet. In the morning, a menacing guard interrogated me in a dingy room lit by a single bulb. On another occasion, guards slapped and punched a female colleague in front of me while they demanded I give up information.

The Air Force does everything in its power to let Airmen experience the sights, sounds, and emotions of standing in the arena. It wants them to taste fear, push through, and realize that their inner strength can take them far beyond what they once thought possible. If an Air Force pilot is shot down and captured today, she will feel tremendous fear, but she will also feel recognition.

A Spartan King once said, "Man differs little from man by nature, but he is best who trains in the hardest school."[48]

Failure is the hardest school of all.

COURAGE

It is no simulation.

Hitting the limits of your personal strength—and coming out the other side—replaces your dread of the unknown with tangible experience. Failure is no longer an ethereal demon prowling your imagination; it is a being you have wrestled with. You know the texture of its leathery skin and the sharpness of its claws.

That familiarity becomes the basis of courage.

You launch your next startup knowing what it will feel like to someday close the doors. You commit to a new relationship despite knowing the pain of a broken heart. You begin your next book knowing it may only ever reach a few dozen readers.

The world has hurt you once.

You survived.

What more can they do?

PRIORITIES

All of us live according to some set of priorities. These priorities dictate how we spend our scarce time, energy, and resources. In subtle and often unconscious ways, they reflect the standards by which we judge our lives.

Some of us focus on first-mountain priorities. We want to get the best possible education, land the ideal career, make money, build a reputation for success, and be popular and well-liked. There is nothing wrong with any of these things; living a wholehearted life requires laying a foundation of healthy relationships, a good education, meaningful work, and financial security.

Others have second-mountain priorities, or at least claim to. These priorities might include faith, family, duty, friendship, close relationships, or creativity. These lists are often aspirational. They reflect our best selves, the people we *want* to be if we can just get past ourselves.

However, most of us actually live by a different code. Our calendars, checking accounts, and screen time loggers all reveal our *real* priorities. We say we value friendship but have to schedule coffee dates three weeks out. We say we value quality time with our children but compulsive screen time spreads through our day like kudzu vine, choking off sunlight and nutrients, swallowing every open space. We say we value faith but scarcely give it a thought between Monday and Saturday. We say we want to build a professional reputation but fritter away our time chasing the next fix of entertainment, quick riches, sex, or fame. Often times, our only priority seems to be staving off boredom.

We fall short of our aspirational priorities for many reasons. In some cases, we are selfish or addicted, and our inner demons get the better of our intentions. Sometimes we are simply exhausted or overwhelmed, and letting ourselves veg out in front of a movie is an act of grace.

Other times, we sacrifice our heartfelt priorities to satisfy others. A demanding parent who will tolerate nothing less than Ivy League excellence. Elders in our church or mosque or synagogue. A needy spouse or clingy friend.

This disconnect between our aspirational and lived priorities indicates an opportunity for personal growth. If we are honest with ourselves, we have been living for the wrong things.

Failure often forces a reckoning.

When you fail, you fall short of the criteria by which you measured your life. You did not achieve that education, build wealth, or win fame (at least the good kind). Even if you claimed spiritual values, it is now glaringly apparent how much you measured yourself by your professional, athletic, or academic success. You have come face-to-face with your deepest internalized values.

Once you recognize this disconnect, you can ask new questions. Have you been living for the right priorities? If not, what priorities *will* you live by? What is the measure of a well-lived life?

These questions do not succumb to easy answers and are never answered with finality. They are alive and dynamic, like little spirits you carry around on your shoulders.

As you press forward into the next chapter of your life, these questions present themselves anew each day. You sit with them in the morning while you drink your coffee and prepare for the awakening world. You ruminate on them in your darker moments when the walls seem to be closing in. You dialog with them every time you meet with an inspiring mentor, witness an extraordinary act of compassion, or do purposeful work.

Every conversation with these questions steers you towards a truer, more noble, and more complete version of yourself.

Failure gives you a preview of your own death. If that sounds dramatic or morbid, it is not; it is one of failure's most precious gifts. Failure forces you to consider your highest values and the legacy you will leave on this earth.

In the end, death is the ultimate failure. Death takes our whole self—body, mind, and soul—to its final limit. We are helpless before its power. Death will not yield to any act of will or strength or intelligence. It interrupts every plan for the future. Goals go unachieved, countries unexplored, races unwon, relationships untended. Death decrees that we cannot be or do all that we sought.

Brushes with death force us to confront the hard truths about our priorities. Almost without exception, survivors of such encounters conclude that their priorities were wrong.

Palliative care nurse Bronnie Ware identifies five wishes expressed by patients in the final weeks of their lives: "(1) I wish I'd had the courage to live a life true to myself, not the life others expected of me. (2) I wish I hadn't worked so hard. (3) I wish I'd had the courage to express my feelings. (4) I wish I had stayed in touch with my friends. (5) I wish that I had let myself be happier."[49]

What unites these five wishes is the recognition that these patients lived by misguided priorities. Too late, the lies are exposed.

Those who brush with death—only to be granted a reprieve—

receive a special gift: the opportunity to consider life, death, and legacy while they still have time.

My dad received such a gift. He spent the first decades of his professional life running his father's business. He was good at it, successful, and well-liked. He made his father proud. However, his truest self yearned for a different trajectory—a fact he had ample time to consider after a drunk driver rocketed through a red light and T-boned his driver's-side door.

I came home from summer camp to find my dad slouched in an easy chair, mottled purple, clad in a neck brace, in pain and struggling to concentrate.

He got better. Within a few years, he quit his job and started the hobby store he had always dreamed of. He worked hard but was fully alive. He taped his personal motto to the cash registers: *Growing old is mandatory; growing up is optional.*

Our family accompanied him on the journey. Mom kept the books and did a thousand errands. Throughout high school I worked at my parents' sides. I have warm memories of late evenings at the store, takeout dinners, decorating after-hours for Christmas, and the shared realization of a dream.

I felt a sense of wholeness in this experience, rooted in my dad's faithfulness to his deepest sense of self.

My mom had her own encounters with mortality when she began volunteering as a chaplain for the local fire department. Time and again, she comforted families coping with the unimaginable.

One December, when I was home for Christmas, she responded to a tragedy that afflicted a family much like ours. The dad—my own father's age—had fallen from a short ladder, hit his head, and died while putting up Christmas decorations. Another time, she joined the disaster response team in the small town of Oso, where a freak mudslide buried 49 homes and 43 people.

I have to think these experiences shaped my mom in ways she herself cannot fully understand. They softened her, opened her world, and expanded her already deep capacity for love and generosity.

Mom and dad thrived in their new midlife roles. Later, after successfully growing and scaling the hobby store, they retired and now live amidst a brood of grandchildren and a strong community of friends.

Peace seemed to settle on them as they grew into themselves, discovered what was most important, and shaped their lives in accordance with that discovery.

Failure can bring a similar reckoning. It challenges us to become people who, in the end, will look back on their lives with satisfaction.

Reevaluating your life priorities has a practical dimension. We are all creatures of habit, and changing ourselves is never easy. Altering how we spend our free time, how we spend our money, or how we relate to others is every bit as challenging as exercising regularly or eating healthier.

James Altucher writes that you are the average of the five people you spend the most time with, the five things you do every day, the five things you think about most often, the five things you do to help others every day, and so forth.[50]

This tool is brilliant because it immediately provides a map of your *real* priorities. Try it out for yourself. Do it in writing. Create one version that is aspirational. Write down who you *want* to spend time with, what inspires you, what you *want* to occupy your thoughts, what you *want* to eat, how you *aspire* to help others. Then write a second version that captures how you actually live.

If your results are as disconcerting as mine, you have learned something invaluable about yourself. You have hard evidence of a disconnect between your stated and your actual priorities, which also provides a roadmap for growth and enrichment. And there is no better time to reorganize your life, reallocate your time, or rekindle old friendships, than in the breaking dawn after this dark night of the soul.

BOUNDARIES

A well-lived life requires constantly growing our personal capacities and limits. However, we must do so wisely.

The key to growth is progressive overload, not running ourselves into the ground. Unfortunately, too many of us do the latter. Society conditions us for it: the cult of productivity, the fierce competition for success, the 24/7 bombardment by emails and texts, the avalanche of responsibilities, the pressure to have a side hustle, the feelings of guilt if we slow down even for a moment.

In the aftermath of failure, we have an opportunity to reflect on how we found ourselves so overstretched. Failure teaches us to reconsider boundaries.

Years ago, when I dreamed of being a Silicon Valley entrepreneur, I secretly envied a young founder I knew. He ducked out of social events to make engineering decisions, close deals, and give directions to his team. He was always in overdrive, always plugged into a creative team that never seemed to sleep.

I admired his participation in an energy field that seemed to pulse invisibly through every atom in the universe. As someone who lacked an outlet for my entrepreneurial ambitions, I could only imagine being plugged into such a dynamic, creative, energetic community.

When I began the Syria Airlift Project, all that changed. My inbox overflowed. I lived on my phone, offering guidance and assigning tasks and conversing with my team. The very idea of boundaries was anathema. I worked hard but had never felt so alive.

Over the months I learned that I had fundamentally missed something. Even as I expertly managed the acute stresses day-by-day, I did insidious long-term damage. The real story of burnout did not play out on a 24-hour cycle, but over months or years.

When you do what I did, you are like an athlete who overtrains. You push yourself harder and harder and harder. You break records and perform incredible feats, but you rack up a long-term toll of torn muscle fiber, weakened joints, and stressed bones. When your performance finally starts to deteriorate, it is too late; recovery will take years, if you are able to recover at all.

Failure makes a mockery of your can-do attitude and inexhaustible strength. Your mistakes become self-correcting. If you do not set boundaries, boundaries will come unbidden: knee pain, writer's block, choking desperation.

You learn to modulate your efforts. The *only* way to build strength over time is through progressive overload: knowing exactly where your boundaries lie at any given moment, and smartly pushing outward. Too slow, and you stagnate. Too fast, and you break down and undermine all your progress.

Setting boundaries does not mean settling for mediocrity. On the contrary, boundaries protect your ability to operate at your absolute best. Boundaries are part and parcel of being at the top of your game, physically, mentally, and emotionally.

There are times to push past boundaries. A desperate wartime battle. A peak athletic performance. A business deal that will make or break a company and determine the fate of a thousand employees. Sometimes you bet all your chips, even knowing what it will do to you.

These must be exceptional occasions, not the rule. If you lend your strength without limit, you will flame out before you achieve your goals. When the hour of need arrives, you will have nothing left to give.

Knowing yourself and your boundaries is essential to wise living and good leadership. You must be a good steward of your own energy in order to be effective, successful, and happy. Once you enter a leadership role, that self-awareness is critical to the example you set.

In a highly motivated team, teaching boundaries is a difficult leadership challenge. Your exceptional subordinates burn with the same passion, commitment, and ambition that you do. They might even burn brighter; they are likely younger and have greater reserves of energy. Your star employees will cook up a new idea at five p.m. on the Friday before Christmas and deliver a working prototype Sunday afternoon. Customers will be thrilled. Your bosses will heap praise on you. Revenue will soar. You will have every incentive to keep pushing, or at least to get out of their way.

And yet.

You have been down this road before. Your superstars might awake each morning feeling chipper and excited to tackle new problems, but you know all too well the demons that will haunt them later: the degraded performance, the chronic fatigue, the restless anxiety, the sick fear of opening the inbox, the sense of loathing when they sit down before a computer screen to write or code.

You know this. They do not.

They are young. They are immortal.

It takes courage to stand before your team and tell them to pace themselves. It takes even more courage to put your money where your mouth is. It is not easy to forego sending that Saturday evening email—even though your boss just gave your team a tasker—because you know it will blow up your subordinate's weekend. It takes self-control to wait a few more days to get that killer feature into production, instead of cramming today.

You are like a wizard cradling a writhing ball of lightning between your fingers. You spread your hands and close them, and watch all that massed energy expand and collapse in on itself. That is your team. Managing this energy, this life force, is one of your most important tasks. You have a responsibility to achieve the highest possible performance from your team, but at the same time you must protect them from themselves—and from you.

You learn all this by going through it, which is why failure is so instructive. You develop a keen understanding of what bestows energy and what robs you of it. You work smarter, not harder. You apply your focused attention like a scalpel.

The space within your boundaries becomes your walled garden. Beyond is the hard and cruel world, the place where you go to fight your battles and slay your dragons. Within is a cultivated space where you spend time with people you care about, and where you sleep untroubled. You fortify the walls with routines to set your mind at ease and soothe your nerves. You might embrace journaling, tea, yoga, CrossFit, or prayer. You might kill every alert on your mobile device, unsubscribe from every marketing email, batch email times, mute Slack, and wean yourself off compulsive news checks. You might say no to requests and taskers that do not align with your sense of purpose.

You have to find your own way through these particulars. Everybody's are different.

When you deliberately cultivate this space within you, the

transformation can be amazing, yet we must be careful. We often think of these as "life hacks" designed to squeeze even more productivity out of our day. Increased productivity may well result, but if we make that our goal, we set ourselves up for a fall.

Organizing our lives within carefully constructed boundaries is not merely a way to increase productivity; it allows us to live integrated lives and serve a resonant purpose, in harmony with the world around us. Good boundaries help us grow into our best selves.

GRATITUDE

I sometimes wonder if it was all worth it.

If I could go back in time, would I make different choices? Would I still go to Stanford? Would I dare to attempt something as noble and foolish as the Syria Airlift Project? Would I found and lead Rogue Squadron, knowing the battles I would need to fight and the constant drain on my happiness? Would I sign up again for the three a.m. anxiety, the crushing weight of responsibility, the months and years of reflection on failure, and the long journey to patch myself up and get back in the arena?

Even now, sitting in the stillness, contemplating all my scars, the answer is immediate and unambiguous: yes. I would do it all again. I am thankful for all of it.

When my oldest son was a year old, we bought him a "thankful for" book. Every night we jotted down one thing he was grateful for. These conversations became a nightly ritual for all three of our children.

Lest you think Wendy and I are saints, we struggle with consistency like every other frazzled, overcommitted parent. Months and sometimes years have gone by without an entry, but it is a practice we always return to in fits and starts.

Our children love flipping back through these dog-eared pages and rediscovering forgotten experiences. Gratitude is a trait we want our children to internalize, and we know that children thrive on routines, especially happy and positive ones. Beyond that, an emerging scientific literature shows that gratitude actually rewires the brain and leads to significant positive outcomes.

I have always known that I should keep a gratitude journal of my own, just as I knew that I should exercise, meditate, eat healthy, work less, spend more time with friends, and sleep more.

I tried here and there, but never consistently. I was too busy to make a habit of gratitude.

I finally began gratitude journaling under odd circumstances.

One day, when I went to pay Rogue Squadron's supporting contractor for another year, I discovered that my parent organization had accidentally "lost" my entire annual budget during a personnel changeover. The three million dollars I needed had already been spent.

I fought many battles while leading Rogue Squadron, but this was unprecedented. Without those funds, I could not pay my people beyond the next two months. The entire team, these guys I loved who worked so hard for me, would lose their jobs and have to scramble for new employment. Rogue Squadron would cease to exist overnight.

For the next week, I stumbled through a red haze of rage. I met with person after person in my organization. Nobody would even acknowledge a mistake. The individual most responsible for the mistake was rude and condescending. I seriously contemplated quitting.

I eventually had to admit that justice would never be served. I could let the anger and bitterness gnaw me apart from the inside or I could somehow transcend it. It was that fundamental principle of Stoicism again.

I opted for self-mastery. I met with the director of my organization, a man I respect and like. He apologized and developed a new funding plan with his internal operations team. It was not ideal, and meant a net loss of almost two million dollars, but it was a generous act under the circumstances that would keep my team employed.

Afterwards, I felt sick and exhausted and spent. By some miracle, my entire calendar was open for the day. As I prepared to head back to work, I caught a glimpse of the mountains in the distance. My heart ached for solitude and nature. I thought, *Why the hell not?*

I drove to Castle Rock State Park, the local rock climbing crag. I hiked around the park, bathing in sunlight and the aroma of ancient towering trees. I sat on cliff edges looking out over spectacular vistas. I found a gnarled cave weathered into one side of a towering rock, where I holed up with my journal. And then I began to write.

I spelled out every angry, anxious, and terrified thought. I wrote about feeling betrayed. I wrote about the worst-case outcomes I feared. I wrote about the people who had wronged me and my team.

Then I did my best to reframe each and every one of those dark thoughts, pouring out gratitude and looking for hidden opportunities in even the darkest places.

Bureaucratic ineptitude had stolen my budget. Reframe: I was grateful for a strong, principled director who supported my team and was willing to discuss further funding in the near future.

I worried about my team losing confidence and fleeing for other employment. Reframe: I was grateful for such a stellar team of mission-focused guys who trusted me and kept working their hardest even when collapse seemed imminent. And so it went.

As the hours passed, and I filled the pages of my notebook with expressions of gratitude and opportunity, the anger and stress drained away. When I returned home that afternoon, I felt better than I had in days. The world was still a hard place, but light burst from its seams.

How you allocate your attention defines how you experience life. Too many of us ruminate. We replay the past, seethe with anger, wrestle with guilt, and resent the obstacles that stand before us. We dissipate vast energies wishing the world could be different, instead of curiously examining the world in search of possibilities and solutions.

A key tenet of mental wellness is gaining intentional control over our attention. Disciplines like meditation and prayer teach us to dial down the noise and gain better awareness of our attention, which we can then focus to experience rich, full lives.

Gratitude channels our attention away from rage or anxiety and helps us to find the subtle goodness woven through every challenge. Like a beam of light sweeping through a dark room, gratitude abolishes negativity. The two cannot coexist. Gratitude is always there for the taking, no matter our circumstances.

A cultivated sense of gratitude can spill over into every part of our lives. A few days after the Stanford fire, when I was still recovering from shell-shock, I sat under a tree one day, too tired to do much of anything. I looked up at the branches flashing bright and green under the sunlight. The sheer majesty of this one tree suddenly overwhelmed me—the slow decoding of DNA into living cells, the growth of those first shoots into sunlight, the magical reversal of entropy as this living wonder unfurled itself in defiance of gravity and the ravages of time.

This single tree was a miracle. One could spend a veritable lifetime exploring its every bend and crease, the fractal unfolding of its branches, the intricate patterning of every leaf, the remarkable internal infrastructure for feeding and pumping and removing waste and harnessing energy. And this was just one modest tree among dozens in our neighborhood.

I wondered what it would be like to experience all of life this way. Even in the midst of failure, one could live an enchanted life, seeing and experiencing a world that blazed with goodness. Life could still be sacred. It could be nothing short of divine.

PERSPECTIVE

Failure forces you to reconsider your most basic understanding of success and failure. Most of us cling to a rather binary definition. One athlete wins a race; the others lose. One product succeeds; another fails. One company thrives and grows while another goes bankrupt. When we begin a new venture, we desperately want to end up on the correct side of the balance sheet.

We hunt for a formula that will guarantee success. We obsess over the lives of great leaders. Entire books offer case studies of market-leading companies, with the implicit promise that if you just follow their methods, you too will succeed.

If you study history, you learn that this is not how innovation works. Organizations, ideas, and individual human beings do not move on linear trajectories of success or failure. The world does not divide into winners and losers.

The truth is so much more complex.

To put your failure into context, let's start with the beginning of the universe.

Near Eastern creation myths tell us the earth was formed out of primeval chaos. Genesis echoes these old religions; the earth "was formless and empty" and "darkness was over the surface of the deep." Modern science has pulled back the curtain, giving us a dazzling view of these primeval beginnings: an explosion of inconceivable scale, an outward surge of spinning matter and energy that is still spreading across the void 13.8 billion years later.

The magnitude of death and destruction at work in interstellar history is inconceivable. Some atoms spiraled off into the infinite void. Others congealed under the blind force of gravity, heating under unimaginable pressures until they ignited into stars. They burned for millions of years, fusing light elements into heavy ones, creating the raw materials of the universe. Then they exploded, scattering stardust across the endless dark. An observer would have seen only the hopeless ruin of a tenuous interstellar order. However, over hundreds of millions of years, all that stellar debris compressed in on itself, forming worlds.

Across this vast universe, across uncountable worlds, molecules collided and broke apart and froze and thawed. Every single collision was a little science experiment. Somewhere, amidst that sea of improbability, a few stuck together. Amino acids formed. Some endured. Replicators emerged. And then, somehow, life began.

Every living organism, from single-celled bacteria to Leonardo da Vinci, is a novel experiment. We usually think of evolution as a biological process, but it is far more than that; it is an algorithm—*the* algorithm—for experimenting, creating, and finding new ways forward in an incredibly complex universe. Every tweak to genetic code explores novel possibilities for life. Most of these experiments lead nowhere and quickly vanish, but all this novelty is the raw material of innovation. Life comes together, reproduces, and combines promising DNA in novel mashups. Every once in a while, life steps in an unprecedented direction, finding a better fit for its environment. The tree of life branches, blossoms, and continues its reach towards the heavens.

Evolution is discomfiting. Untold millions of organisms die for every successful adaptation. Most variations result in deformity or death. Nature is red in tooth and claw, as predators seek their prey, playing their assigned part in complex food chains that undergird the whole biological world. The flourishing ecosystem we see today, teeming with verdant life and its rich variety of creatures, is only the tip of a submerged iceberg.

And now we reach the tiniest sliver of time, the millisecond before midnight on the cosmic clock: human civilization. The same evolutionary process that birthed the universe and the tree of life applies to human beings and their creations.

Prehistoric men and women fashioned crude tools, watched them break, and gave up in frustration. Others came along, saw the ruined pieces, and envisioned improvements. They experimented with different forms of governance: tribes, chiefs, dictatorships, democracies. Governments rose and fell. Wars tore down old orders and gave rise to new ones. Mankind experimented with different means of organizing labor. Companies came and went. A company became a dynasty only to collapse a generation later; its grizzled veterans went out into the world to found their own companies, make their own unique twists, and yield a new generation of technology. They found each other, formed partnerships, and created new mashups of old ideas.

We would never use words like failure or success to describe individual notes in this cosmic symphony. We only see this marvelous unfolding of order, creation and destruction in a dance as old as the universe.

The economist Joseph Schumpeter described capitalism as "gales of creative destruction." It is not just capitalism. Every economic system, every political structure, every community, and every human endeavor is an evolutionary experiment.

Schumpeter's quote sounds frightening at first. It means we have far less control than we think. But if we really understand it, it also liberates us. Success and failure are not one-time events. They are both parts of the ongoing process that animates the universe.

Each action you take plants seeds in this wild, vibrant, evolutionary jungle. Every investment in a colleague or subordinate could shape that person's life. Your discarded creative projects become building blocks for the next generation, or for your own future efforts. Work you abandoned will surface in entirely new places, changed and yet mysteriously familiar. Lessons you learned long ago will help you avert catastrophic mistakes in the future.

This view of the world becomes almost comforting. You are not such a big deal after all, and that is okay. You faithfully play your part in the cosmic symphony. You make investments, plant seeds, and cast your bets on steps towards a better future. How much you plant will define your legacy.

This takes patience.

Your legacy may not be apparent for years, if ever. Many talented, devoted people never see the fruit of their labors in their lifetimes. You cannot live with the expectation that your work will be redeemed; that only sets you up for disappointment. You must let today be enough, and then delight when one of your scattered seeds unexpectedly blooms.

A few weeks ago, I stumbled across the eclectic personal website of Chris Crawford, a game designer who has spent decades trying to improve the state of interactive fiction. A recent post titled "Forty Years of Failure" inventories his lack of accomplishments.[51] He has bounced from one dead end to another. His ideas never took hold, and only a few dozen people regularly follow his blog. Even so, Chris keeps showing up. He keeps writing. Over a lifetime he has assembled a treasure trove of deep thinking about interactive storytelling, and he generously shares his wealth of knowledge with the world. Chris knows that many inventors live before their time. That hope propels him onward.

I think Chris is right. I eagerly await the day when some graduate student or video game designer stumbles across that website and reads until dawn, feeding her own intuition, working her way towards the breakthrough that Chris always sought.

Chris bravely takes the long view.

Taking the long view changes how you approach daily life.

First, you learn to view both successes and setbacks as mere milestones on a much longer journey. Any cause worth fighting for will be a winding road with many ups and downs. That holds true whether you pursue universal health care, quantum computing, interplanetary space travel, racial equality, or the renewal of your local community.

Second, once you realize how tenuous success and failure can be, you look for joy and purpose at a level deeper. Far from draining your energy away from your work, this reprioritization enriches and energizes it. Teddy Roosevelt, between seasons of fiercely combative politics, spent long months in the Montana wilderness ranching and enjoying his hobbies. Winston Churchill had his oil painting. Each of us has spouses, children, parents, friends, or lovers who infuse our lives with purpose, meaning, and value. We can live full, rich lives that transcend the successes or failures of the day.

Third, even as you pursue your biggest dreams, you learn to plant other seeds and cultivate opportunities along the way. You invest in the people you work with. You help them achieve their own goals and dreams. Even if everything else hits the fan, you can rest assured that your legacy will live on through these exemplary human beings.

One of my quiet joys of the past few years has been watching my volunteers and employees thrive in new ventures. Jessie, Uplift's Vice Director, developed a reputation for leadership and expertise in the drone sector. Airbus hired her to lead a rapid innovation team. Brandon, our Director of Engineering, was accepted into a prestigious leadership development program at Northrop Grumman. Adam, one of my other volunteers, followed me to Rogue Squadron, where he was instrumental in building and leading a new team.

Uplift is only a memory now, but these stories bring everything full circle. They show that nothing given generously and wholeheartedly in this world is ever wasted.

POWER

In 2001 I began rock climbing at Garden of the Gods in Colorado Springs. From the air these red rock towers look like the plated back of some primeval dinosaur, half-submerged beneath the foothills of Colorado's Front Range.

Although I mostly climbed the easiest rocks, the rush was exhilarating. The red sandstone was warm beneath my fingers. I felt the sun and breeze and cool sweat. Every muscle fiber felt alive, attuned to the requirements of each sequence. Tourists congregated to watch. I felt strong and capable.

Mixed with that sense of power was utter fear. Even on these stumpy rocks, I struggled to make many moves. My arms pumped out quickly. I did not trust my feet. I often felt sick with vertigo. My legs shook violently. I had terrifying visions of the rope snapping, or the anchor breaking loose, sending me smashing to the broken rocks below.

One day my friend Ray and I climbed Montezuma Tower, a two-pitch shark fin looming above the middle of the park. My parents were visiting and watched nervously from the base.

At the top, as we prepared to rappel back down, I threaded the rope incorrectly through my belay device. Ray caught my mistake at the last minute, saving my life. If I had gone over the edge, I would have decked at the feet of my parents.

I descended uneventfully.

Hours later, reflecting on that moment, an abyss of terror

opened within me. I did not climb again for eighteen years.

I never expected to take up rock climbing again. I had no desire to expose myself to that kind of danger.

Then, in December 2018, at a time when I was under immense pressure leading Rogue Squadron, I watched *The Dawn Wall*—a documentary capturing Tommy Caldwell's and Kevin Jorgenson's extraordinary ascent of the hardest big wall climb in the world. Climbers had been scaling Yosemite Valley's legendary El Capitan since 1958, but everyone assumed free climbing the blank face of the Dawn Wall was impossible—until Caldwell proved everyone wrong.

The film captivated me. What struck me was not the climb itself but Tommy Caldwell's inner journey that made this achievement possible. In 2000, while climbing in Kyrgyzstan, Caldwell and his climbing partners were kidnapped by terrorists. They escaped only after Caldwell pushed a captor off a cliff, which led to years of guilt (much later, Caldwell learned his captor survived). Despite these traumas—or rather, because of them—Caldwell's fear evaporated. As he described it in interviews, he found a fire inside. His experience taught him that people are capable of so much more than they imagine.

Later, Caldwell lost his left index finger in an accident with a table saw. A severed finger would have ended the careers of most climbers, but not Caldwell. After his rehabilitation he knocked out one elite climb after another, exceeding his previous abilities.

Later, he underwent a devastating divorce. Failure kept coming for Caldwell, but he refused to succumb. He found the strength to regroup and applied all his burning intensity to the Dawn Wall. Year after year he returned to that blank granite face, exploring every centimeter, mapping every hold, mastering the details that would enable his breakthrough climb.

What really impressed me is how Caldwell's hardships deepened his fundamental perspective on life. The movie hinges on a critical moment when he successfully climbs the hardest pitch of the Dawn Wall and has the opportunity to finally complete the ascent he has dreamed of for years. Instead, with the finish in sight, all he can think about is his partner, who is still stuck on the hard pitch below. Completing the climb without Jorgenson would be a hollow victory. Caldwell backs off from his imminent victory, returns to his hanging tent, and reunites with Jorgenson.

Over the next few days Caldwell glows with relaxed confidence as they work to complete the pitch and finish the ascent together. He does not rush. He is a man at peace with himself and the world. He knows what is important in life. This stunning documentary about rock climbing has suddenly become a film about friendship and values.

That is power, I thought.

Not ego. Not arrogance. Not achievement. On the contrary, power is the quiet, confident self-mastery to push past one's own limits every single day—while not being overly attached to oneself or the achievement. Power means feeling secure enough to look past yourself and live for what matters—for your values and for other people.

I wanted what Tommy had.

Eighteen years after that near-miss in Garden of the Gods, I started climbing again. I set a goal I have only confessed to a few people: I wanted to someday climb The Nose, an iconic climb up the 3,000' prow of El Capitan.

I picked this goal because it seemed impossible. Although The Nose was far easier than the Dawn Wall, it still entailed climbing thirty pitches at mind-boggling heights, with terrifying exposure. It required incredible strength, toughness, and technical skill. Many experienced climbers consider the Nose a lifetime achievement, and half the climbers who start up the route have to bail. I had not climbed since college, was almost 40, and possessed none of the requisite skills. Fear overwhelmed me when I climbed three feet off the ground.

But Tommy Caldwell's story ignited something in me.

My goal was audacious but possible—*if* I dedicated years to patient, steady, incremental improvement. I would have to push myself in ways I never imagined possible. I would have to confront fear every day. As I emerged from my season of failure, so desperately tired of being afraid, that sounded attractive.

My first efforts made a clumsy and laughable contrast to my epic goal. On my first day at a climbing gym, I quickly exhausted myself on the easiest boulders. My hands blistered and bled. I struggled to put on my harness correctly. An employee reprimanded me for bad techniques I had picked up in college. Chastened, I unlearned bad habits and started over.

I stuck with it.

Arno Ilgner's book *The Rock Warrior's Way* shaped my journey. Ilgner argues that the warrior spirit is about the impeccable use of attention. A trained warrior focuses attention to perform "with absolute mastery and calm in the face of mortal danger."[52] A warrior's lifelong quest is to gain the self-knowledge and personal power necessary to focus attention.

This philosophy creates a paradigm for understanding training, both in rock climbing and life: "Essentially a warrior is an *impeccable hunter of personal power*. He gains power by taking forays into the unknown where he focuses his attention, grapples with chaos, and learns from the experience."[53] Warriors do not seek power over others but themselves.

If your goal is to continually expand your personal power, then success and failure become almost irrelevant. Each provide opportunities to learn lessons that will increase your personal power and give you more mastery over the future. In fact, failure offers the most growth.

Ilgner gave me language to frame every step of my journey. I needed to spend as much time as possible at the frontier of my abilities—never lingering in the comfortable middle—setting and pursuing small goals. My task that first day was not to climb El Capitan but to master putting on a harness. My circle of personal power, however small, grew larger.

I have steadily gained personal power since then. I climbed often. I set micro-goals like learning to flag or backstep. I advanced grades. I completed a lead climbing course in my gym. I took a series of outdoor classes, working my way up to outdoor lead climbs. I was afraid every time I climbed but learned to manage the fear.

Like most meaningful ventures in life, it is hard to see progress day by day. The gains are too small to notice, but when I look back over the months, the progress is warmly satisfying.

Coronavirus wreaked havoc on my spring training plans. Yosemite and other parks closed, killing my plans to learn crack, multipitch, and trad climbing. The Air Force relocated me to Alabama, which is not renowned for its mountains. The nearest climbing gym is 90 minutes away.

In keeping with Ilgner's philosophy, I focused my attention on possibilities. I turned my garage into a climbing gym, which, though tiny, forced me to emphasize strength over fun. The lack of a real gym pushed me outdoors; every other week or so, I make a six-hour round trip to northern Alabama where I now climb progressively harder and scarier climbs. I recently started "trad" climbing, a rigorous and frightening style of climbing that I would need on El Cap. This spring I intend to tackle multipitch and aid climbing.

El Capitan still looms somewhere out there on the horizon, only glimpsed occasionally through the clouds. I have no idea when or how I will climb it, but after two years of disciplined effort, the goal is no longer crazy; it is very much within reach. Dierdre Wolownick, who I wrote about earlier, became the oldest woman to climb The Nose at age 66. She started like I did, from the beginning. I am hopeful.

Each day I focus on more proximate goals. I am playing the long game. As long as I keep pushing myself and expanding my personal power, my warrior spirit will continue its ascent.

Once this concept clicks, it changes how you live your life. Every struggle becomes a welcome opportunity to learn, grow, and break through personal limits.

For the last twenty years I have been a comfortable and complacent skier, enjoying sunny days on lazy intermediate runs. This season my kids begged me to take them down a black diamond. I seized up. I had never skied a black diamond. I feared injury. I worried about my kids. As I pondered the decision, I realized that avoiding a growth opportunity directly contradicted the values I was internalizing through my climbing.

Off we went. We soon found ourselves on the steepest mogul field I had ever skied. We inched and tumbled our way down the run. Skis flew one way, poles another. My kids cried with frustration. I was miserable. We licked our wounds, returned the next day, and tried again. We did much better. Now black diamonds are routine for us. My kids led me through the greatest ski breakthrough of my life.

The warrior mindset goes well beyond action sports. It is fundamentally about your attitude towards limits. Each of us must make choices about how to handle our fear of what lies beyond our comfort zone. Too many of us content ourselves with the status quo. We are terrified to approach the edge of what might be possible.

As a warrior, you commit to embrace this unknown. Fear becomes a welcome teacher. Every time you feel that prickle on the back of your neck, you recognize that an opportunity stands before you. Each encounter with fear invites you to confront your own limits and push forward into new possibilities.

Your experience of failure steeled you for these moments of decision. It taught you that you can endure more than you ever imagined, painful though it might be. You can live an entire lifetime on the very edge of your limits. Sometimes you will succeed. Sometimes you will fail. You will get hurt. You will be humbled. But you will always, *always* learn and gain further mastery over yourself.

As your personal power grows, you will continually face the ultimate question: what you will do with it.

LOVE

It was love that brought you here.

That is why failure hurt so much.

You loved your career, your revolutionary idea, your creative masterpiece, your sport, your university, your spouse, your friend, your child. That is why you gave so much, so generously, for so long.

In the end, your love was not enough. Failure still came for you. Whatever happened, your heart was broken, and you spent all this time healing.

Now, as you contemplate the future, you wonder if you will ever love again.

If you even dare.

My pace of life in Rogue Squadron was relentless. If I was lucky, I could squeeze in a brief period of reflection and journaling in the morning. Once the phone rang or the first email arrived, the onslaught did not stop until evening. Each day included a constant barrage of meeting stakeholders, guiding subordinates, putting out fires, and making key decisions.

Late some afternoons, when my meetings finally came to an end, I dropped into the lab. The team would not even notice me because they were too busy working. I would kick back in my chair and put my heels up and just watch. Ash, Mark, and Pieter debated some new software architecture tradeoff in our counter-drone server. Adam was on the phone recruiting Silicon Valley's best and brightest. Thomas, William, and Beau laughed as they updated software on the sensors we were building. Jon, Jeremy, and Dan were dialed in from abroad. I heard James and Dillon in the back room, repairing hardware.

Magic unfolded around me. Ryan and I had made plenty of mistakes as leaders but somehow, amazingly, these guys had become a team. They enacted our vision together, inventing and improving and riffing off each other's work.

Some days the guys demoed entirely new capabilities that we had never even asked for. On one occasion, an entire product team disappeared to a rental house. They reemerged a week later with a vastly improved design.

The team's surging performance gave me a minor identity crisis. In the early days, I had written code and designed products. I was too busy for that now. As I delegated more to the growing team, I became less and less sure of my role. However, on those days when I had no idea what to do with myself, I felt something unexpected: love.

I loved these guys. I loved their magic of creation. I loved their collaboration, arguments, and technical negotiations playing out on every whiteboard. I loved the constant joking. I loved that our Texas conservatives and California liberals were good friends. I loved the fact that every single afternoon the team went for a "Rogue walk", which entailed encircling a nearby building and idly tossing a football.

That is what kept me going in the hardest job I've ever had.

I did it for the love.

It is a strange thing, learning to love again after failure.

You are guarded. You know what it feels like to give too much of yourself, and do not want to be devastated a second time. The minute those grand feelings swell in your breast, you panic. Your instinct is to back off from commitment.

However, a life without commitments is no life at all. Anything worth doing requires commitment, and that entails risk. It means giving something of yourself, even with the knowledge that you might be hurt again.

You have a choice to make. You can stay in the shadows where it is safe, but only at the cost of growing, creating, giving, sharing, and loving. On the other hand, you can step out in faith and vulnerability. You can willingly embrace the risk of the unknown because that is what love asks.

Love does, however, become wiser after failure.

We live out this arc in our romantic relationships. When we are young, we often give our love to illusions. We become infatuated with superficial caricatures of that guy or girl at school, or dream of a Hollywood romance. We expect marriage to solve our unhappiness and loneliness. Somewhere along the way we discover that life does not quite work like this. Real relationships take considerably more effort. They are infinitely more textured than Hollywood would have us believe. Real love requires long engagement with the endless complexity of a real human being.

The same is true of anything you give your heart to. You might imagine yourself as the next Steve Jobs or Elon Musk and follow the gold rush west to Silicon Valley to found your startup. You might dream that your debut novel will make you the next Neil Gaiman or that your basketball talent will make you the next Michael Jordan. Your love is superficial.

Failure burns that naive idealism out of you and clears space for real love to grow. You come to understand the work entailed in making this relationship succeed. Failure puts your love to the test; it asks you to carry a load.

You might discover that your love does not run as deep as you thought. There is no shame in that. You learned something valuable about yourself and can move on with your life enriched by the experience.

Then again, maybe you do feel ready to commit to years of difficult work with no certain reward. Elizabeth Gilbert, the author of *Eat Pray Love*, knew at a young age that she wanted to be a writer. She had no idea whether she would succeed financially—most writers don't—but she told herself, "I'm marrying this." Gilbert made a deal with her writing: "I will never ask you to support me financially. I will always support you. I will work hard so that you can play lightly."[54]

That is love.

The day will come when you love again.

Your next venture might echo your past. I recently caught up with a friend who commanded an Air Force squadron. It did not go well; his leadership style crashed and burned. As he grappled with this failure, the Air Force granted him a rare opportunity: a second squadron command. Armed with newfound humility and wisdom, he led well. He redeemed his past and emerged a better and wiser leader. I am delighted for him and his Airmen.

You might walk away from your past entirely. You might set out in a different direction: a new career, a new relationship, a new hobby or activity. You will test unfamiliar waters and suddenly find yourself swept away in a new adventure. I think of our Uplift volunteers, who are all doing marvelous things in a wide variety of careers even as they marry, have kids, enjoy friendships, and live their lives.

Personally, I never want to look at a drone again. That baffles most of my colleagues, who know the success I could find in the industry. I am not interested. I loved Uplift. I loved Rogue

Squadron. But my heart has moved on.

You might also take your time here, not rushing into anything new. Life will carry you along. You will relax into the flow. You will accept the small graces as they come. Love will find you in the quiet in-between moments, which might be the most important moments of all.

One day you will wake up and realize the alchemy is complete; whatever you just endured no longer seems like failure. You might reject the language of success and failure altogether. There is just life, with all its wild ups and downs, its brilliant offerings of success and its careening plunges into self-doubt and despair. If you are like me, you might experience both every single day, sometimes simultaneously.

It has been quite a journey.

What you experienced in this season will repeat throughout your life in big ways and small. The dance between soaring expectations, brokenness and disappointment, healing, and growth never ends. It gets easier, or at least more familiar. You break in your life like a pair of old slippers. When each season comes around again, you greet it like an old friend.

So where do you go from here?

Go do what you love. Do it with the people you love. Stay humble, stay open, stay attentive. Always listen. Reflect. When failure strikes, do not let it break you; let it break you open. When success propels you forward, be grateful, humble, and generous. If you feel stuck, know that every season passes. In the meantime, let the process teach you what it has to teach. May you grow in wisdom, compassion, and kindness. May your power grow. May you go back out renewed and strengthened to take on the world.

AFTERWORD

Around the time I finished the first draft of this book, fortune played one more hand.

Rogue Squadron was succeeding wildly. We saw exponential demand and were deploying a drone detection network that made generational leaps over other DoD efforts. I had a huge vision for what Rogue Squadron could achieve. I began pitching an actionable plan for expanding our network to nearly every major DoD base in the world.

However, even as we navigated this exponential growth, Ryan and I faced a critical problem. The resource we most needed was the one resource we didn't control: ourselves.

DoD's talent management system made it almost impossible to keep a high-performing team together. Imagine founding a startup in which the CEO and all executives are forced out every two years, with no ability to choose their replacements. That was our dilemma.

Ryan was probably the top small drone engineering expert in the United States government, but the Navy passed him over for promotion twice because he had been leading Rogue Squadron instead of flying helicopters like the Navy expected him to. That triggered an automatic process to separate him from active duty.

For my part, I was due to transition to a new assignment on SAASS faculty. I agonized over my dilemma. I loved SAASS, owed the school a teaching payback assignment in exchange for my PhD, and felt an ethical duty to fulfill my commitment. However, I saw Rogue's situation as exceptional. We faced a make-or-break moment; we could deliver a DoD-wide breakthrough, but if Ryan and I left simultaneously, the team would collapse.

One of the innovators we studied at SAASS was General Bernard Schriever, who spent five years in California architecting the United States' Intercontinental Ballistic Missile Program in the 1950s. It was one of the greatest revolutions in airpower since the invention of the airplane. If SAASS exempted my teaching payback, maybe, just maybe, I could do something similar for counter-drone efforts. To pay back my PhD commitment, I could guest-teach part-time until I retired.

I approached SAASS leadership with my request.

The response was firm: it was time to come home.

I spent anguished months exploring any lead that might save Rogue Squadron. This season began to feel like my last months in Uplift, when I frantically juggled increasingly desperate contingency plans. I criss-crossed the country, visiting organizations and evaluating potential leaders. I saw no viable options.

Ryan and I were determined to shut Rogue Squadron down rather than let it become mediocre. As the clock wound down, that looked like the most likely outcome.

At the eleventh hour, a new option materialized. A different U.S. government team I'll simply call The Organization expressed interest in acquiring Rogue Squadron. The Organization was highly placed, had an insurgent ethos like our team, and hired Silicon Valley misfits who liked to deliver software capability at blistering speeds.

We spent months planning the merger together. As soon as Ryan separated from the Navy, The Organization would hire him as a government civilian to provide leadership continuity. I would have four months of overlap to manage the transition and would continue to consult from SAASS. With Ryan still leading the team within such a supportive organization, Rogue would have everything it needed to survive and flourish.

I was nervous but bursting with hope.

For two years I had feared another failure like Uplift. This time would be different.

The merger went into effect.

The Organization's first act was to remove me, reversing our agreement for a months-long changeover. Before they even finalized my removal, they broke contact with me and began communicating through my subordinates, which wreaked havoc in my team. It was less a firing than an excommunication.

The Organization also failed to hire Ryan as promised, leaving him unexpectedly unemployed for two months—while paying Silicon Valley rent, with a young family—after his expulsion from the Navy. A few months later, they fired our talent manager.

The Organization replaced my product managers without telling them. They decreed sweeping changes to technical projects they did not understand. They casually cut off key customers, including an allied nation that fielded our technology at scale. Our horrified allies reached out to me for help, but it was too late.

The evisceration of everything we had built in the previous two and a half years was breathtaking. I could not have planned a better assassination if I tried.

When The Organization's director gave me a tepid farewell at an all-hands meeting, he asked if I had any final words.

I looked out over the sea of faces. I said, "Take care of my guys, or I'll hunt you down."

Here I am again. A two-time failure now.

It's not really a failure, especially this time. I just like to be provocative.

The team we built did immense good in its time. The Department of Defense, with its soulless 1950s bureaucracy so finely tuned to steamroll over innovation, simply had no capacity to appreciate what we had built. Ryan and I did what hard-charging military officers have done since the beginning of time: do as much good as they can before the system runs them over. That is how the system continues to function at all.

But if you go with the more personal definition of failure—of being stretched past one's breaking point—then yes, I found myself riding out failure's cycle a second time.

Ryan and I gave everything we had. We burned with love and devotion to a cause and our team. We drew on every last scrap of knowledge we had, every relationship, every skill, every insurgent trick we knew. In the end, it was not enough.

The other members of Rogue Squadron are each on their own journey now. Some have moved on. Many are still at The Organization. A year later, the turmoil has mostly settled down. My guys still fight for success, still support many of our customers, and still try to create positive change inside the broken Pentagon. I am incredibly proud of them.

Rogue Squadron still exists, as do many of our projects. However, my vision is a lost memory. Rogue Squadron is no longer the team I built, and it is certainly not the team I wanted it to become.

I am getting better at handling failure.

After I pledged to hunt down The Organization's director, I went to my car and cried. Only for a few minutes this time, a considerable improvement over the agonizing weeks when Uplift was failing.

AFTERWORD

Then I called Ryan. We vented a bit. We reflected on how we had missed the warning signs and made such a devastating mistake. We talked about the future. We both felt grief, but we also felt that a weight had lifted from our shoulders. Life would not hold us down for long. We spun plans for what might come next.

I thought of Tommy Caldwell sawing off his finger. He wasted no time getting back on the rock.

It was 10:15 in the morning. I had no responsibilities. Not today, not anytime soon.

I went to a coffee shop, opened my notebook, and made a list of all the ways I could use this newfound gift of time. I wanted to write a memoir about my time leading the team. Get back into writing fiction. Build a personal website. Start a business. Learn some new technology frameworks. Practice writing business plans. Call old friends. Rock climb. Finish this book.

Dr. Tyrell tells his short-lived synthetic humans in *Blade Runner*, "Revel in your time." It is a fine motto.

It was surreal, reading and rewriting every section of this book in the months that followed. I discovered that no lesson could ever be fully learned. Each section held fresh meaning in light of my new experience.

The negative emotions of failure are still sharp and real. Deep anger always lies just beneath the surface. I can conjure it up in an instant, if I wish. My chest tightens. My hands curl into fists. My heart pounds. A torrent of black thoughts gushes forth: anger I did not receive more support, the hurt of betrayal, righteous indignation at Rogue's fate. I feel robbed of my life's work.

I often grapple with feelings of futility. Every major professional endeavor of my life has ended in disappointment. I wonder why I bother, why I care so much. I second-guess myself constantly. I inventory my strengths and weaknesses, dwelling more on the latter, wondering what is wrong with me that I keep making these kinds of mistakes. Every time I try to write, anxiety paralyzes me. I worry about oversharing.

I turned 40 a few months ago and am close to retirement from the military. Most of my friends have risen to the pinnacles of their careers. My Air Force friends now command Squadrons and Wings. My Uplift volunteers are excelling in the private sector. Ryan landed an important and lucrative job leading a drone development team in private industry. Some of my junior developers now earn twice what I do. I keep watching their careers take off, little spaceships activating their warp drives and shooting off into the stars in streaks of light.

Then there is me.

I have careened from one realm of expertise to another, never staying long enough to feel like I found success. I struggle to maintain a stable sense of identity. The tide washes away every castle I build. Many mornings I sit at my desk, staring into space, wondering who I am and who I am supposed to be.

And yet I have been through all this before, and the lessons failure taught me the first time around are always close at hand. My own written reflections on healing and growth serve as gentle reminders of the path before me.

I know I have choices to make. Down one path lies a lifetime of bitterness and regret; down the other lies new life, peace with the past, and hope for the future. I know which way I will go, even if I get lost along the way sometimes.

I have been at SAASS for six months now and am finally hitting my stride. SAASS is the only place in the Air Force I have ever felt at home. I have a more relaxed pace of life, with abundant time to think and write. I love my colleagues.

My relationship with SAASS has always been complicated, but I try not to dwell on that. It's like a marriage; there is strength in commitment. In a lasting marriage, you learn to roll with the hurts because your love goes deeper. I am grateful for the opportunity to think, teach, read, and write. At this point, I have a lot to say. My life's work will simply have to change.

I love mentoring a rising generation of leaders. It's fun, teaching a classroom full of Majors and Lieutenant Colonels everything I know about being a loyal insurgent inside government. I require each of my students to pitch an innovation proposal, and their expertise, talent, and creativity consistently awe me. I keep planting seeds, and keep trusting that they will go forth and lead change. Our country and our world desperately need what they have to offer.

I diligently work to apply my own insights. I still write in my gratitude journal. I still practice my discipline of reframing anxieties. I try to be less self-centered, worry less about my future, and spend more time being generous and helpful to others. I make myself sit down and write each day—not just because I want to be a successful writer, but because I know that sharing my journey with others is a generous act.

I did not break sieges in Syria with drones or build a global drone detection network. I did not become an Air Force commander. I did not publish my dissertation, or even a journal article. I have turned down opportunity after opportunity to do what I felt was right, go where I thought I could have impact, and follow where my heart led me. Along the way I have, at least, become somewhat wiser. I have learned to fail. I have learned to rise again. I am doing my best to share those lessons with others.

That is enough for today.

Learn more and sign up for my newsletter at
www.markdjacobsen.com

As an independent author, I rely heavily on word-of-mouth to tell the world that my books exist. If you like *Eating Glass*, I invite you to tell your friends or leave reviews on sites like Amazon and Goodreads.

I also love hearing from my readers. If *Eating Glass* speaks to you, drop me a note through my website!

ACKNOWLEDGEMENTS

This was a hard book to write and an even harder book to release into the wild. I owe a tremendous debt to many people.

John Schiavone read my first reflections and urged me to expand them into a book. *Eating Glass* would not exist without his gentle prodding. Sam Sundquist kept vigil with me during the hardest times, encouraged me through the rest of my PhD, and believed in the book and my writing ability when I doubted both. Emily and Elliott Leigh, Brandon Fetroe, Jessie Mooberry, Kevin Wells, Adam Hesch, Jamil Musa, Brian Lee, Anthony Kappus, Jeff Decker, Eric Knudtson, Ryan Beall, and David Willard also came alongside me in critical ways.

Anything good that I achieved during the last five years can be credited directly to the amazing people who worked to realize my first, uncertain visions. The volunteers at Uplift Aeronautics were amazing. You performed miracles. There are too many of you to name individually, and I also want to respect your privacy, as I know each of you has made your peace with that experience in different ways. Just know that your individual names and faces— and the contributions you each made—are flashing through my mind as I write this. You continue to do amazing things, and I hope your lives were in some way enriched by the time you volunteered with Uplift.

My fellow Stanford PhD students provided indispensable encouragement throughout my three-year grind. I am also thankful to my dissertation advisor and committee for getting me across the finish line. It was a rollercoaster, compounded by an inner journey that you couldn't have known about, but I never doubted your earnest commitment to helping me finish and graduate.

Three generations of leaders at DIU (formerly DIUx)—Raj Shah, Sean Heritage, and Mike Brown—enthusiastically supported my innovation efforts. DIU's Autonomy portfolio, led by Jameson Darby, provided a home and protective screen within the organization. The Autonomy PMs were the best teammates I could have imagined, and the entire DIU internal ops team worked tirelessly to support Rogue Squadron's unique requirements. As for "my guys" in Rogue Squadron, leading you was an honor and privilege.

I am grateful to my colleagues at the School of Advanced Air & Space Studies (SAASS), my home in the Air Force. You have given me a home where I can think, write, and educate a rising generation of leaders. I take that responsibility seriously, and hope this book—however unconventional—contributes to the school's mission of preparing strategists and leaders. Three successive commandants made my unique journey possible: Timothy "Astro" Cullen, Shawn "Johnny" Cochran, and Jeff "Push" Donnithorne. I am especially thankful to Push for giving me his blessing to tell my story.

Several authors guided me through my journey, although I have never met any of them: David Whyte, Jerry Colonna, Parker Palmer, David Brooks, Steven Pressfield, and Ryan Holiday. Readers who found value in *Eating Glass* should read them next.

My bedrock through this season was my family.

I am thankful to my parents, Bob and Laurie, and my sisters Robyn and Alley and their families. No matter how far I journeyed from familiar shores, I knew I was never beyond your love and support.

ACKNOWLEDGEMENTS

My children Isaiah, Mariam, and Colin are my greatest delights in this world. Tickle time, morning cuddles, and Saturday donuts and park visits brought great joy through many hard weeks. When the day comes—many years from now—that you find yourselves lost in a metaphorical wood, I hope you will dust off this book and find wisdom here.

To Wendy: you are my love, my best friend, and my greatest treasure. I marvel each day that I am married to such a strong, determined, and fearless woman. I am eternally grateful for you.

REFERENCES

[1] Lewis, Sarah, *The Rise: Creativity, The Gift of Failure, and the Search for Mastery* (New York, N.Y: Simon & Schuster, 2014), 11-12.

[2] Freeman, Michael. "Are Entrepreneurs Touched by Fire?" Pre-Publication Manuscript, 2015, https://michaelafreemanmd.com/Research_files/Are%20Entrepreneurs%20Touched%20with%20Fire-summary.pdf

[3] Pain, Elisabeth. "Graduate students need more mental health support, study highlights," *Science*, March 6, 208, https://www.sciencemag.org/careers/2018/03/graduate-students-need-more-mental-health-support-new-study-highlights; Katia Levecque, Frederik Anseel, Alain De Beuckelaer, Johan Van der Heyden, Lydia Gisle,

"Work organization and mental health problems in PhD students", *Research Policy*, Vol 46 No 4, 207, https://www.sciencedirect.com/science/article/abs/pii/S0048733317300422

[4] Rosin, Hanna, "The Silicon Valley Suicides", *The Atlantic*, December, 2015, https://www.theatlantic.com/magazine/archive/2015/12/the-silicon-valley-suicides/413140/

[5] "A Year of Hardship in Yarmouk", United Nations Relief and Works Agency for Palestine Refugees in the Near East, https://www.unrwa.org/newsroom/photos/year-hardship-yarmouk

[6] Pressfield, Steven, *The War of Art: Break Through the Blocks and Win Your Inner Creative Battles* (New York, NY: Black Irish

Entertainment, 2002)

[7] Both videos are available at markdjacobsen.com/http://markdjacobsen.com/uplift-aeronautics/

[8] Weiss, Scott, "We're F****D, It's Over: Coming Back from the Brink", Scott Weis, March 24, 2014, https://scott.a16z.com/2014/03/24/were-fd-its-over-coming-back-from-the-brink/

[9] Myers, Meghan, "Army report: Self-doubt and sleep deprivation led to 2-star's suicide", Army Times, January 11, 2017, https://www.armytimes.com/news/your-army/2017/01/11/army-report-self-doubt-and-sleep-deprivation-led-to-2-star-s-suicide/

[10] Busse, Brendan, "Andrew Garfield played a Jesuit in Silence, but he didn't expect to fall in love with Jesus", America Magazine, January 10, 2017, http://www.americamagazine.org/issue/grace-enough

[11] Harris, Joshua, "'I Kissed Dating Goodbye' author: How and why I've rethought dating and purity culture", USA Today, November 23, 2018, https://www.usatoday.com/story/opinion/voices/2018/11/23/christianity-kissed-dating-goodbye-relationships-sex-book-column/2071273002/

[12] Harris, Joshua, "A Statement on *I Kissed Dating Goodbye*", Josh Harris Personal Website, https://joshharris.com/statement/

[13] Harris, Joshua, "'I Kissed Dating Goodbye' author: How and why I've rethought dating and purity culture", USA Today, November 23, 2018, https://www.usatoday.com/story/opinion/voices/2018/11/23/christianity-kissed-dating-goodbye-relationships-sex-book-column/2071273002/

[14] "Burnout." *Merriam-Webster Dictionary*, https://www.merriam-webster.com/dictionary/burnout

[15] Glouberman, Dina, *The Joy of Burnout* (Skyros Books, 2013), Kindle Loc. 1289.

[16] Whyte, David, *Crossing the Unknown Sea: Work as a Pilgrimage of Identity* (New York, NY: Riverhead Books, 2001), 132.

[17] "Reboot Podcast Episode #125 - The Grief of Closing Down the Business - with Avni Patel Thompson", Reboot, May 29, 2020, https://www.reboot.io/episode/125-the-grief-of-shutting-down-the-business-with-avni-patel-thompson/

[18] Lewis, C.S, *The Great Divorce* (New York, NY: 1975), 20-21.

[19] Bacon, Lance M., "Airship maker sues Navy after roof collapse disaster", Navy Times, March 14, 2015, https://www.navytimes.com/news/your-navy/2015/03/14/airship-maker-sues-navy-after-roof-collapse-disaster/

[20] Strassler, Robert B. (ed.), *The Landmark Herodotus: The Histories* (New York, NY: Random House, 2009), VII.33.1.

[21] Day, Elizabeth, "S8 Ep6, How to Fail: Glennon Doyle", How to Fail podcast, July 8, 2020, https://howtofail.podbean.com/e/how-to-fail-glennon-doyle/, 49:00.

[22] Kornfield, Jack, *The Wise Heart: A Guide to the Universal Teachings of Buddhist Psychology* (New York, N.Y.: Random House, 2008), p. 17

[23] Hollis, James, *What Matters Most: Living a More Considered Life* (New York, N.Y.: Gotham Books, 2009), Kindle Loc. 86.

[24] Burns, Stewart, ""Cosmic Companionship: Martin Luther King Jr.'s Lived Theology", April 3, 2018, To the Mountaintop, https://martinlutherking2018.com/2018/04/03/stewart-burns-cosmic-companionship-martin-luther-king-jr-s-lived-theology-in-lewis-v-baldwin-and-victor-anderson-eds-revives-my-soul-again-fortress-press-forthcomin/

[25] Khan, Pir Villayat Inayat, *Thinking Like the Universe: The Sufi Path of Awakening* (New York, NY: Harper Collins, 2000)

[26] St. John of the Cross, *Dark Night of the Soul*, http://www.carmelitemonks.org/Vocation/DarkNight-StJohnoftheCross.pdf, 33.

[27] Holiday, Ryan, *Stillness is the Key* (New York, N.Y.: Penguin,

2019), 7.

[28] Dillard, Annie, *Teaching a Stone to Talk: Expeditions and Encounters*, New York: Harper Perennial, 1982).

[29] McRaven, William H, "Adm. McRaven Urges Graduates to Find Courage to Change the World", UT News, May 16, 2014, https://news.utexas.edu/2014/05/16/mcraven-urges-graduates-to-find-courage-to-change-the-world/

[30] "Constitution", World Health Organization, https://www.who.int/about/who-we-are/constitution

[31] "The Ottowa Charter for Health Promotion", World Health Organization, 1986, https://www.who.int/healthpromotion/conferences/previous/ottawa/en/

[32] Schiavone, John, "On Returning to Stanford", October 25, 2016, https://learningconnection.stanford.edu/john-schiavone-returning-stanford

[33] "Disillusion." *Merriam-Webster Dictionary*, https://www.merriam-webster.com/dictionary/disillusion

[34] Lamott, Anne, *Small Victories: Spotting Improbable Moments of Grace* (New York, NY: Riverhead Books, 2014), 6.

[35] Publisher's remarks on Schwartz, Barry, *The Paradox of Choice: Why More Is Less* (New York, NY: Harper Perennial, 2004), https://www.behavioraleconomics.com/resources/books/the-paradox-of-choice-why-more-is-less-barry-schwartz/

[36] Rockhill, Gabriel, "Unraveling Love Stories", New York Times, February 13, 2017, https://www.nytimes.com/2017/02/13/opinion/unraveling-love-stories.html

[37] Glouberman, Dina, *The Joy of Burnout* (Skyros Books, 2013), Kindle Loc. 979.

[38] Hagerty, Barbara Bradley, *Life Reimagined: The Science, Art, and Opportunity of Midlife* (New York, N.Y.: Riverhead Books), 312.

[39] Rohr, Richard, *Falling Upward: A Spirituality for the Two Halves*

REFERENCES

of Life (San Francisco, CA: Jossey-Bass, 2011).

[40] Brooks, David, *The Second Mountain: The Quest for a Moral Life* (New York, NY: Random House, 2019).

[41] Lewis, C.S., *Voyage of the Dawn Treader* (New York, NY: HarperCollins), 1980.

[42] Holiday, Ryan, *Ego is the Enemy* (New York, NY: Penguin, 2016), 5.

[43] I came across this quote in a book but cannot recall where, and now I cannot find it in Epictetus' writings. It may be a paraphrase or a loose translation but does capture the essence of Stoic thought.

[44] Dio Cassius 72.36.4, Loeb edition translated E. Cary. Cited by McIntosh, Matthew, "Lucius Aurelius Commodus: A Supersized Ego and the End of the Pax Romana", Brewminate, April 28, 2020, https://brewminate.com/lucius-aurelius-commodus-a-supersized-ego-and-the-end-of-the-pax-romana/

[45] Kim, Eugene, "Jeff Bezos to employees: 'One day, Amazon will fail' but our job is to delay it as long as possible", November 15, 2018, https://www.cnbc.com/2018/11/15/bezos-tells-employees-one-day-amazon-will-fail-and-to-stay-hungry.html

[46] Sun Tzu, *The Art of War*, Lionel Giles translation, I:26, http://classics.mit.edu/Tzu/artwar.html

[47] Horowitz, Ben, "What's The Most Difficult CEO Skill? Managing Your Own Psychology", Andreessen Horowitz, https://a16z.com/2011/03/31/whats-the-most-difficult-ceo-skill-managing-your-own-psychology/

[48] Lendon, J.E., *Soldiers and Ghosts: A History of Battle in Classical Antiquity* (New York, NY: Yale University, 2005), 110.

[49] Ware, Bronnie, "Regrets of the Dying", Bronnie Ware, https://bronnieware.com/blog/regrets-of-the-dying/

[50] Altucher, James. *Reinvent Yourself* (Choose Yourself Media,

2017). 20.

[51] Crawford, Chris, "Forty Years of Failure", May 29, 2019, http://www.erasmatazz.com/personal/self/forty-years-of-failure.html

[52] Ilgner, Arno, *The Rock Warrior's Way: Mental Training for Climbers* (La Vergne, TN: Desiderata Institute, 2003), 328.

[53] Ilgner, Arno, *The Rock Warrior's Way: Mental Training for Climbers* (La Vergne, TN: Desiderata Institute, 2003), 357.

[54] "Unlocking Your Creativity", Evolving Wisdom, https://evolvingwisdom.com/blog/unlocking-your-creativity/

www.ingramcontent.com/pod-product-compliance
Lightning Source LLC
Chambersburg PA
CBHW020037120526
44589CB00032B/396